Aligning Values and Politics

Empowerment versus Entitlement

Michael Gendre and Nicolás Sánchez

University Press of America,® Inc.
Lanham • Boulder • New York • Toronto • Plymouth, UK

Copyright © 2016 by University Press of America,® Inc.
4501 Forbes Boulevard, Suite 200, Lanham, Maryland 20706
UPA Acquisitions Department (301) 459-3366

Unit A, Whitacre Mews, 26-34 Stannary Street,
London SE11 4AB, United Kingdom

Library of Congress Control Number: 2015959382
ISBN: 978-0-7618-6723-4 (pbk : alk. paper)—ISBN: 978-0-7618-6724-1 (electronic)

The Paradoxical Commandments are reprinted by permission of the author. © Copyright
Kent M. Keith 1968, renewed 2001. www.paradoxicalcommandments.com.

∞™ The paper used in this publication meets the minimum requirements of American
National Standard for Information Sciences Permanence of Paper for Printed Library
Materials, ANSI/NISO Z39.48-1992.

To the memory of my parents,
Simone M. and Jacques A. Gendre

Michael Gendre

To the memory of my parents,
Blanca E. and Pedro P. Sánchez,
who had the vision to send me to the USA
as part of the Pedro Pan program

Nicolás Sánchez

Contents

Preface

Michael Gendre

This is a book about the interactions between government institutions and the people of the United States, and it is written for a general audience. It was conceived with the goal of explaining to the public why we face serious political conflicts within the United States in the 21st century, and what we must do to resolve these conflicts. From my perspective, many of our problems are grounded in our unwillingness to tackle ethical issues and our disinclination to accept well established economic propositions. We need to align our values with our politics, if we are to bring about positive change to our society. Hence, the reader of this book will have to be willing to gain awareness of forgotten ethical norms, and reconsider the economic consequences of the institutional arrangements that we all take for granted. I am a professional philosopher who has taught ethics for most of my academic life, and my co-author is a professional economist who specializes on the ramifications of institutional arrangements. We are amply qualified to tackle the goal that we have set for ourselves.

The idea and the writing of this book spanned almost three years, from the spring of 2012 to the winter of 2015. Professor Nicolás Sánchez originally came up to me with the offer of a collaborative work after a presentation he made in May 2012 on themes, topics and methodologies included in his book *Destined for Failure: American Prosperity in the Age of Bailouts*. Although I had known Nicolás a little more than two years because of our mutual participation in the Boston-based group Citizens for Limited Taxation, I immediately felt that his presentation to an audience of non-specialists was tackling topics of economics and market behavior in very surprising and enlightening ways. So I gladly accepted his offer to explore the ethical foundations of economic prosperity and good governance in a joint scholarly effort. Almost three years later, in early 2015, our work was finally completed. I am deeply appreciative of the fruitful collaboration that made this book possible.

The scholarly backdrop within which we both agreed to carry on our analyses is the moral and political philosophy of Immanuel Kant. His ideas of good will and respect of the civil independence of others are paramount values expressed in our book. We were also going to explore various historical dimensions of the Western ideas for ethics, but we thought it was important to adopt an open methodology that was congruent with economics. It seemed to us that a reliable rule of law yields short, middle and long-term benefits not only for economic prosperity, but also for the overall well-being of individuals and their communities. It was obvious to us that uncertainty about, or constant tinkering with, regulations have negative effects on individuals, their communities and the culture at large. "The more corrupt the state, the more it legislates," according to Tacitus, a historian of the Roman Empire. But equally important, the moral foundation of American success in the world (sometimes referred to as American exceptionalism) has been gradually eroded. We decided it was crucial to restate how our moral foundations could be rebuilt, and how these new foundations would impact our political discourse.

One stepping stone in that effort was the work of Hannah Arendt, with which I was familiar and which opened up the possibility of sharing with Nicolás her assessment of freedom in the context of mass ideologies. He agreed that *On Revolution* and also other of her works, including *The Origins of Totalitarianism* and *The Human Condition*, were important critiques of those complacencies within the omnipotent state—at home bandying "progress" and "happiness," while abroad letting loose schemes of domination and control which would lead to the hatred of all Western values.

The result of the November 2012 U.S. presidential election surprised us to the extent that several years of massive government interference in the American economy (by both Republican and Democratic administrations) had not sufficiently soured the electorate on costly government bailouts, on the real costs and consequences of subsidizing government programs, and on a newly devised and non-transparent foreign policy of "leading from behind." The foundations for economic prosperity in a rapidly changing technological world, and for accountability in government, were far from being achieved. The imperial schemes of Russia and Iran, along with the flashpoints of ideology of an Islamic caliphate in a global war—and the misguided responses that such events drew from the American administration—made us explore the disconnect between political correctness and the realities felt by the electorate.

More recently, we were influenced by the realization that the federal intrusion into American education—the Common Core experiment—was being challenged across the states for what it was, a partnership of big testing agencies and a bureaucratic class intent on manipulating and controlling—through high-stakes testing—children, their parents, teachers, the municipalities and their taxpayers. The characterization of Common Core as a "bigotry of lower expectations" by able advocates of the Massachusetts superior standards—especially independent researchers at The Pioneer Institute of Boston—hit a nerve with us. Why would ever Massachusetts adopt these lower, untested, non-rigorous standards when that state had achieved superior performance across the board, nationally and internationally? Why should any state become the whipping boy for a poorly and secretly designed (as well as untested) program? This undemocratic experiment is now affecting the lives and pocketbooks of every person, adult and child in the public school districts of the nation; yet the major stakeholders have rarely been consulted.

Our orientation toward the critique of contemporary American governance in terms of a bloated, omnipotent and imperialistic system of excessive government was also prompted by some important themes covered in the last three years by Dinesh D'Souza, a critic of the current administration. Although generally sympathetic with D'Souza's advocacy of freedom, wealth creation and economic benevolence generated by American free market enterprise, we both felt that his arguments were too partisan, and only partially addressed the decades-long malaise of governmental intrusion. We decided to emphasize in our analysis the issue of an electorate that did not know history, economics, or even ethics. Our approach is far more balanced, and is also critical of both political parties.

I was assisted in the task of searching for the cultural roots of freedom by two complementary sources: First, I owe a debt of gratitude to Daniel Hannan's book *Inventing Freedom: How the English-Speaking Peoples Made the Modern World,* which traces the fight of the British against absolutism and tyranny—a process of opposing the imperial overreach begun during the Roman presence in the British Isles and continued when English native institutions gradually recovered from the Norman conquest. The American Founding Fathers benefitted from knowing this historical experience.

Second, seeking additional documentary evidence for Hannan's thesis, I found on YouTube a wealth of support coming from British sources, and in a format—truth to be told!—more engrossing than the reading of books. All of it was owed to teams or individuals commissioned by the BBC, especially but not exclusively BBC 4's *Time Team.* Such research groups and individuals have done, and are still doing, outstanding archaeological work on prehistoric, ancient and more modern sites.

The historical evidence needed for my research would have been hardly possible in the age prior to the late 20th and early 21st centuries, which witnessed the arrival of modern geophysics, the computer and the Internet. But naturally, it needed to be channeled within the framework of an ethical, political and constitutional perspective. Such prospect was always at the ready for me, and it was owed to my academic background. My teaching philosophy and ethics for many years has paid off. I can now relate ancient teachings more accurately to the day-to-day problems of our modern world. For instance, Aristotle would agree that a general principle of duty binds us to our promises, which we still need to keep. Kant would repeat, if he were alive, the centrality of the good will in understanding how the principles of duty can still lead us to virtuous behavior. Epictetus would insist on an ethics of responsibility, which remains relevant to this very day. These themes help us recover the ethical norms that we need to succeed in the modern world!

It is true that in this book we produce arguments in favor of wealth creation that connect private property and the management of skills of just about any kind—if we are free to explore the world and learn from our mistakes as well as from our successes. In no way have we sought, or accepted, to be limited to just one line of thinking. On the contrary, we hold that an ethic of responsibility opens up both our own self-actualization and that of others. That is why it becomes imperative to continue the reconstruction of a frazzled ethical tradition and reconnect these fragments to essential tenets of the Bill of Rights and the American Constitution—thereby showing our American compatriots they have the ability to redress some wrongs that have been in the making for quite some time.

It was and it remains our belief that the American experience wouldn't be worth living if we didn't examine the roots of the Western civilization that shaped it. Doing so allows us to articulate how, from our American perspective, we can still measure up and influence the world in a positive way. Aligning our values and our politics not only serves to strengthen the nation in which we live, but it can make a significant difference in elections for the foreseeable future.

Acknowledgments

We thank Barbara Anderson and Francis (Chip) Faulkner for creating the forum (as part of *Citizens for Limited Taxation* in Massachusetts) where most of the governing issues of the book were conceived and discussed. We also thank *The Pioneer Institute of Boston* for its groundbreaking work on educational issues. This work would not have been possible without the outstanding education the authors received from Boston College, Stanford University, the University of Southern California and California State Polytechnic University, Pomona.

Michael Gendre thanks Wayne Froman, his former colleague at the Collegium Phaenomenologicum, in Perugia, Italy for giving him the impetus to be bold in stating the obvious while daring the new. He owes much to ethical, legal and pedagogical discussions he had with Professors Hector Agostini and Jim Grenier of Middlesex Community College in Massachusetts. Jim Avallon provided unfailing encouragement to make this project successful.

Nicolas Sánchez thanks his former colleagues Charles H. Anderton, John R. Carter, Victor A. Matheson, Kolleen J. Rask and David J. Schap for the many economic discussions that led him to think about the issues covered in this book. He recalls with fondness the students in his Economic Development course who put up with six-hour midterm exams, trying to grapple with some of the economic issues in the work.

Both authors thank Roxana Sánchez for her tremendous assistance in the editing of the text, although they take full responsibility for all the errors that may remain. She has been a source of inspiration and guidance to the authors.

Chapter One

Introduction

Empowering People through Institutional Change

When we empower people, we are providing them with the means for self-actualization. Education is one such means, but so are institutions that allow people to achieve their full potential. Regrettably, people can be distracted from their goal of self-actualization; in fact, many existing institutional structures lead people astray and prevent them from seeking and achieving their human potential.

This book, then, has three objectives. First, we want to make people—our fellow citizens but also perhaps people beyond—aware of the many distractions that influence their behavior and prevent them from achieving their human potential. Second, we provide readers with the historical background and analysis that explains what has gone wrong with our values, economic policies and politics in general. Third, we lay out a positive agenda for creating institutional structures that favors human development and success.

This is not a political book that follows a particular party line; however, we recognize that in order to create new opportunities that empower people, they have to become engaged in the political process and demand the type of change that neither Democrats nor Republicans appear ready to provide. Hence, when we argue that the government usurps our authority, we are blaming both Democrats and Republicans for bad government.

Let's make clear that bad government does not mean ineffective government; in fact, the government is the main culprit in distracting all of us from achieving our latent abilities. The government is quite effective in preventing us from reaching our full potential. We, the people, waste time when we get tangled up in arguing for or against the government's agenda, which has little to do with achieving our self-actualization. If we want change, we need to take a hard look at our values and our behavior, accept that change is necessary, and plan accordingly.

People who are committed to taking sides on various governmental policies will find it difficult to accept our arguments. Both the right and the left (which jockey for supremacy in government) believe that the policies they advocate will make a difference for the people of this country. We disagree. If the reader is already committed to a political party, we ask him or her to give us the benefit of the doubt, and at least consider and respond to the challenges that we present in this book.

The vast majority of people belong neither to the right nor the left, and we want to get their attention. We challenge them because our thesis is that they are being manipulated by the powers-that-be, and no one likes to be told: Wake-up and take control over your life! The people in the political center are wasting their precious time accepting the current political and institutional structures in which they live. Indeed, they get to do a lot of things that they like, but that is not self-actualization!

Self-actualization means achieving the person's human potential, and not simply living a lifestyle of pleasure and contentment. The reader can take this as a not-so-veiled criticism of what passes to be the main gist of the Libertarian political agenda, too.

We recognize that people have likes and dislikes that drive them, in part, towards specific goals. What we are saying is that self-actualization is much more central to the core of a human being than living the happy life. With the appropriate set of institutional structures, both leftists and rightists could achieve far more personal goals, and stop wasting their time trying to impose their vision of the happy life (which is not necessarily the good life!) on the rest of the population. The right and the left are wasting the time of people in the political center.

These people in the political center—who represent our main concern—can be successful in achieving self-actualization. To do so, they have to bury forever, in their political discourse, reference to victims and victimizers, happy and unhappy lives; instead, they have to talk about achieving meaningful lives. They need to take a closer look at their values. Contrary to a claim by Jeremy Bentham, it is not the case that the greatest happiness of the greatest number is the measure of right and wrong. Rather, it is right to treat people as ends, and not as means of creating utopian visions; and it is wrong to prevent them from reaching their self-actualization. Has the achievement of "happiness" become a deviant activity that deserves our concern? We address this issue throughout the book.

The book is organized as follows. Chapter 2 details how the government manipulates people by means of "bread and circuses," and how people come to believe that happiness and personal satisfaction should rule their behavior; regrettably, this approach to life has negative consequences for everyone.

Why has this happened? We blame the growth of a manipulative government on the self-interest of the elites, who manipulate people by means of distractions. Most people fall for these distractions, as we try to demonstrate.

Chapter 3, then, explains the role that government institutions should play in our lives, from a philosophical point of view. It justifies limited, rather than all-inclusive government. Regrettably, the American educational system is such that many are unaware of the historical road that the West has travelled when it comes to government, and we use this history to articulate both the positive and the negative roles that governments can and do play.

However, even if we make the case that limited government is justified, this does not guarantee a well-functioning state. While it is true that our own democracy has been subverted in the past decades by the "bread and circuses" discussed in Chapter 2, we need to develop a system of values that not simply promotes self-actualization, but that promotes civic duties, cooperation among peoples and the advancement of economic growth. These are the topics of the next two chapters, as follows.

Chapter 4 takes a hard look at our moral values, and develops the fundamental principles of duty. Many readers will find this chapter challenging because most, we suspect, lack any training at all in ethics, and do not even remember—let alone understand—President Kennedy's simple injunction "Ask not what your country can do for you, ask what you can do for your country." If we are seriously going to confront the problems that we face as a nation, which are not just economic but ethical in character, we have to become acquainted with ethical theory, and we urge our readers to consider adopting the ethics proposed by the great German philosopher Immanuel Kant. We are particularly impressed with his thought because it allows us, in subsequent chapters, to tie together ethical duties with both economic issues and public policies.

Chapter 5 tries to resolve an apparent contradiction between the two previous chapters. Chapter 3 argued for limited government, while Chapter 4 argued for taking seriously our personal duties. But, do our personal duties require an active and enlarged role for government? The answer is no, but to make our case a convincing one we need to draw a clear line between self-actualization and the principles of duty. In order to do so, we first argue that the right to private property is an aid in the fulfillment of freedom, and then explain the role that insurance plays in resolving problems that most individuals think can only be solved by an all-powerful governmental authority. It will become clear that insurance schemes and limited government can fit together harmoniously in the presence of private property rights. This chapter also provides a penetrating analysis of slavery, which further helps to clarify our duties and the role of government.

Regrettably, many people believe that the existence of private property rights and ethical values are conflicting norms. This is not the case because private property rights expand our opportunities as human beings, allowing us to achieve self-actualization. Chapter 6 acknowledges that historically speaking, the ownership of property (particularly land) led to oppression. But it then argues that the problem was not the ownership of property itself, but rather the restraints that rulers imposed on the acquisition of property by others.

However, we will admit that inheritance presents special difficulties in the creation of a just and well-functioning society. Hence we propose a unique set of rules of inheritance in Chapter 7 that demonstrate our willingness to transcend the goals of conservative and liberal ideologies. This chapter will likely raise disturbing reactions in most readers, for it will challenge either their conservative or their liberal expectations. Yet our conclusions followed from the logic that we had developed.

Chapter 8 continues with another challenge, when we take up the highly controversial topic of abortion and try to resolve it with a similar non-partisan analysis.

Chapter 9 brings to the fore the conflict between empowering people versus giving them entitlements, analyzing how free markets work. It begins with an analysis of taxation and the political process, concluding with the surprising idea that free and competitive markets end up reducing conflict in society. While we argue that free markets create income disparities, these can become acceptable within a framework of an existing safety net, and the acceptance of philosophical values that justify self-actualization.

Chapter 10 argues that even the highly emotional topic of discrimination can be handled within a free market economy. Discriminatory behavior can be eliminated permanently by market forces, rather than by political arrangements. Also, people need to become aware that supporting the tax status of the nonprofit sector has negative consequences for most citizens, as we shall explain.

Chapter 11 puts together the historical and philosophical background of property relationships. We believe that history justifies our belief in the positive role that private property can play in a well-functioning society. However, we also note that the traditional conception of property changed significantly in the 19th and 20th centuries, when the separation of ownership and control over corporate property became important. This had consequences in the political field because it allowed the corporate elites to partner with the state in imperialist enterprises, which subverted the positive role that private property could play in many countries.

The next five chapters try to re-legitimize government and unfold a positive agenda for change. Chapter 12 discusses the limited success of recent social movements in America (such as the Tea Party, Occupy Wall Street and Black Lives Matter), followed by the extraordinary difficulty of getting Constitutional amendments approved. We try to explain what we can learn from these efforts.

Now, since changes require a strategy, we propose in Chapter 13 that we must first re-ratify our Constitution, and then accept or reject a large number of interpretations that have been imposed on the body politic by the Supreme Court's judicial activism. We also propose six extremely imaginative constitutional amendments, which will surprise the readers.

We then argue in Chapter 14 that, despite our best intentions, we face many obstacles when we try to change our institutions. We argue that people have a natural inclination to accept the status quo, and even in a democracy we face many constraints regarding what can be accomplished. Some of the obstacles can be overcome with a different treatment of legal tender in America and prevention, both at home and abroad, of drastic changes in the value of currencies. Libertarians will be pleased with our analysis.

There is one constraint, however, that we do not face, but many people misunderstand. Who is the creator of our own wealth? The answer is simple: We are. And we do so by developing the appropriate technologies, using markets to achieve specialization, developing institutions that support private property rights, and creating a government that brings about both domestic and international peace. We also consider the many actions that destroy wealth or delay its creation. These are the topics found in Chapter 15.

Some governments, however, do not trust the domestic sources that lead to wealth creation; instead, they choose to practice imperialism, which attempts not to create wealth, but rather to transfer wealth. That is the central concern of Chapter 16. We demonstrate how imperialism was rampant in Europe and was later adopted by the United States government. The subject of imperialism has become passé in America, but people must become aware that it has deep roots in Western history and that we are once again practicing it. We are not conscious that we are currently following an old catastrophic trajectory that has a negative impact on governance and welfare within our country.

Our concluding Chapter 17 is a plea for sanity in our modern world. We, as a society, have abandoned a traditional respect and concern for ethical values, and these must be re-introduced and internalized within ourselves. We are on the verge of disaster not only because we do not understand how we can create and make use of wealth, but also because we possess no useful purpose, except that of making people "happy." The ethical values that we advocate will create a sense of purpose for ourselves and for our institutions. We demonstrate that individualism and altruism are mutually compatible. We emphasize the need for participation and debate in the political process, taking into account the connections that exist between personal and civic duties. We urge readers to be beneficent and charitable towards others. We want people to achieve personal empowerment, rather than depend upon entitlements to reach the illusion that they have found happiness. But all of these goals require institutional change.

Modern ethical values can no longer be justified on authority; they need to be justified by the evidence that rightfully comes from taking care of oneself and from being encouraged to be pro-actively involved in an altruistic ethics of care. We do not offer anything spectacularly new to the reader, except a reminder that the ethical values we support are part of our Western heritage: Ethical norms must be rediscovered. If we don't, our dream of achieving empowerment will not come about and, most likely, subsequent nightmares will be harder to dispel.

The afterword and summary by Nicolás Sánchez explains why an economist had to accept ethical values as central to the analysis of the problems that we face in the United States, and provides a summary of the main findings of this book. We urge readers to contact us and engage us in the discussion that we have started.

The book concludes with three appendices that explain several scholarly assumptions that the authors made, their conception of what scholarship is about, and the context of the Kantian texts as well as the subsequent use of Kant's philosophy by well-known scholars and philosophers. These appendices are not central to the main text but complement it.

Chapter Two

Manipulating People
by Means of "Bread and Circuses;"
Then and Now

Most educated people are aware that the Roman Republic was succeeded by the Roman Empire in the century before the birth of Christ. One century later, the Roman poet and satirist Juvenal made reference to "bread and circuses," to point out that his fellow Romans cared no longer for political involvement and were instead appeased and distracted by cheap food and entertainment.[1] Civic duty among the common folk of the Roman Empire was all but forgotten. Have we reached a similar historical junction in the political life of the American Republic? Or even worse, do governments at various levels use bread and circuses, plus more, as a means of social and political control?

There is no doubt that in America we have lots of available and cheap food; but not just food acquired through personal income generated in the labor market, but rather food provided through subsidized food stamps or Electronic Benefits Transfer (EBT) cards made available by the states and the federal government. The US population increased approximately by 35 percent between 1983 and 2014 (from 236 million to 319 million) yet the Supplemental Nutrition Assistance Programs (food stamps) increased by 582 percent in nominal terms; in real terms (after accounting for inflation) the figure is 193 percent, which is no paltry increase.[2] Note that this period includes both Democratic and Republican administrations.

As of December 2012, 35 percent of the population in America received subsidies from one or more means-tested government programs, which included (besides food stamps or their equivalent) free or reduced lunch and breakfast, energy assistance, state-administered supplementary security income, Medicaid and additions to veterans' benefits (not included under "veterans' compensation"). This figure of 35 percent also does not encompass another 14 percent of the population that received benefits to which they had at least partially contributed, such as social security, veterans' benefits, unemployment compensation and Medicare. This situation is no different now.

The main goal of this chapter, however, is not simply to expose the data, but rather to argue that it is in the nature of government to try to entice people to their side, and appease some of their gripes, by means of food and entertainment which is subsidized. Most people are aware of EBT cards and food subsidies, but have no awareness of subsidized entertainment. The equivalent of Roman circuses has taken on different characteristics and attributes throughout the centuries, yet the roles that they have played in governance are easier to understand when we look back in time, rather than when we look at their equivalent modern institutions from a current perspective. People are prone to believe that others in the past could be easily fooled: but they themselves, somehow, cannot be manipulated. We disagree.

We explore the past to make our case convincing. The running of the bulls in Pamplona (which supposedly goes back for over five centuries) is now reported on television news when someone is gored; the event is part of the San Fermin festivities in Spain. The run draws international attention because the event seems both farcical and absurd: Who on Earth would like to be run over or be gored by a bull? Furthermore, the event is unique . . . but is it?

The Corrida de Toros is known as "bullfighting" to English speakers. Yet the Spanish phrase "corrida de toros" (meaning literally "running of the bulls") is known in Spanish as "Encierros," which occur when the bulls are moved from the countryside to the towns. The most famous "corridas" in Spain, besides the San Fermin festivities, are the Encierros de Cuellar (dating all the way back to the 13th century), the Encierro de San Sebastián de los Reyes (in Madrid), the nocturnal run in Navalcarnero (which is especially dangerous), the run in the town of Tafalla, and many others. The bulls are still run not just in Spain, but also in Portugal, Southern France, Mexico and Peru. Bulls were run in Stamford, England, for almost 700 years, but the runs were abandoned in 1837. In the old days, street runners used arrows and darts to try to maim or kill the bulls—often ending up maiming or killing the spectators!

These popular activities were and are promoted by the state. Bullrings for "bullfighting" were owned outright by state and local authorities, or by groups representing associations with significant governing roles and influence. They were subsidized by members of royal families, who had a stake in the success of the government as a ruling enterprise. What difference, then, is there between the bullring plazas of years past and the stadiums of modern times?

Promoters of sport events claim that these stadiums promote the local economies, with little empirical evidence to that effect.[3] Besides, even if a local economy is benefited by a bullring plaza or a modern stadium, one has to understand that the surrounding areas lose income when people from nearby and afar travel to attend these entertaining events. Political leaders are the ones who have the most to gain from these sporting events, for they provide a rather mindless form of entertainment and distraction, similar to what was achieved in the circus performances of Roman times.

Let us add the obvious about our modern "circuses." Baseball in America is formally exempted from antitrust legislation.[4] In addition, the federal government rarely interferes in the workings of sport team organizations, for successful sports require close-enough contests and competitive degrees of performance between teams. Otherwise, the events become boring. Balanced team performances have to be arranged by collusive practices; if not, the wealthy teams (attracting the best players) would always win. Sports organizations control entrance into their markets, and do so with government support. An eatery or clothing store cannot prevent competition, but sports organizations have the power to control the number of teams that are allowed in the marketplace. While sports stadiums are formally subsidized, people forget that the institutional structure of sports competition leads to higher income for sports teams.

The same analysis applies to college sports teams. The one difference is that the federal government has allowed professional players to unionize and demand high salaries, whereas college players rarely receive compensation; and when they do under the table, the national organizations penalize the colleges that fail to police the cartel arrangements that they themselves created.

The public does not perceive or understand that professional and college teams are detrimental to the public in a variety of ways. People only perceive the positive effects of cartel practices. Cartels (associations which act as monopolies, despite having several members) serve as a sieve that guarantees high performance among players, but they make it quite difficult to introduce change into an industry. There is no reason whatsoever, for example, why baseball has to be played the same way year after year. Change comes to baseball after painful and long delays, such as the change in the height of the pitchers' mound.

There are three distinctive reasons why sport cartels are damaging. The most obvious is that cartels prevent price competition, making the sport events far costlier to fans. The second is that they distort the schedule of compensation to players (which in sports involve both salary and income from publicity). As a result, too many students try out for college teams and too many of them take excessive risks in trying to reach professional levels. The media fail to report innumerable failure cases due to injuries of all types, an underreporting that enables the media to promote sports as a glamorous activity.

The third is far more severe and perverse, and results from the adulation and notoriety that sports figures achieve. Young people come to believe that watching college and professional games somehow enhances their worth as individuals. Sadly, human beings get satisfaction from living vicarious lives. The problem is compounded when we have an educational system that is simply unwilling to rank performances publicly, and the young come to believe that everything they do is up to par with the best performers (thereby being able to relate to both college and professional athletes). In summary, the institutional structure of college and professional sports leads young people astray regarding their own potential.

In 2014, Major League Baseball had 73.6 million people in attendance. In 2013/14, the National Hockey League had 22.3 million in attendance; the National Basketball Association had 21.4 million in attendance; and the National Football League had 17.4 million in attendance at regular games. (All these numbers are available in the Internet or World Wide Web, if the reader searches for the umbrella organization for each sport.) We realize that these numbers do not include the many, many more millions watching the games on television and other mobile devices, but that strengthens the point that we are about to make.

If we add these numbers (134.7 million people in attendance) and multiply them by 3 man hours per game, we get the man hours spent on games by people in attendance, which is 404.1 million man-hours. Furthermore, when we multiply these figures by 8 (our own minimal estimate of the number of people watching the same games on television), we get the astonishing number of 3.2 billion man-hours devoted to watching four major professional sports in America during the course of one year! This figure excludes mobile devices, which could easily add another billion man-hours to the total.

Readers should note that we have not even bothered to account for the millions of young people (and other adults) watching college sports in person or via television and mobile devices; our educated guess is that the wasted human potential is far worse than previously indicated. In addition, some of the sports lead to significant gambling activities, which take up additional time. All this wasted time could be used for the self-improvement of the spectators' human capital, or at the very least help others to improve their human capital.

Now, when you tell a person in America (and especially when you tell a young college student in America) that poverty could be greatly diminished if people watching sports would devote half the above man-hours to helping the poor improve their reading and writing skills, they become visibly shocked, angry and disturbed, arguing back that it is not their obligation to watch fewer games. These young people claim that it behooves the government to transfer more money to the poor; the poor are the responsibility of the government, period. (The authors of this book believe that college and university faculty have given up asking their students to stop watching college and professional sports, even when the faculty holds morally responsible beliefs.)

Similar arguments hold true for parents of younger children, who think that their offspring are going to be successful athletes or singers or dancers or actors on television and elsewhere. Parents seem to spend far more time than other fans (of college and professional events) watching sports, music, and theatrical performances of atrocious quality when their children are growing up. These parents are not only wasting time: they are actually misleading their children about their true potential, for a miniscule number of these children will end up with careers in those professions.

Equally surprising, parents see no connection between their behavior and the assistance that they could—but fail to—provide to the poor or those in need of personal assistance. To many of them, it is always the government that has to do the heavy lifting among the poor and those with special needs. The consequence of this parental behavior is that elementary, secondary and college faculty are put through the ringer and have to teach the mastery of subjects to students who have no interest in learning about other fields, because they are distracted by—and greatly taken by—sports, music and theatrical performances either live or on television.

Simultaneously, the government (either through example, such as inviting professional athletes and entertainers to the White House and/or through the promotion of sport games and dreadful artistic performances in the public schools) is doing next to nothing to promote excellence in education. Instead, it is creating a continuing aura for circuses that either appease or distract the public into a rigmarole of staged contention.

However, the government goes far beyond creating distractions. It formally engages in the control of citizens. We already mentioned one type of control, via the public educational system. Whereas in years past there were state educational controls, which were mitigated by the existing competition among local and state authorities and the direct supervision of parents, the funding mechanisms of the federal government have gone into high gear to achieve national control of education. While population grew from 1983 to 2014 by 35 percent, federal discretionary educational expenditures grew by 856 percent. To put the money figures in real terms, we must add that the inflation index went from 1.00 to 2.30; therefore, the increase in expenditures far exceeded the increase in prices.[5]

The new and direct method that is being used by the federal government to control the educational process is through the Common Core Curriculum, which demands minimal educational standards in all states. This curriculum was sponsored by the National Governors Association and the Council of

Chief State School Officers, and it was developed with the assistance of the Bill and Melinda Gates Foundation, the Pearson Publishing Company, the Charles Stewart Mott Foundation and others. The Common Core Curriculum received federal support through the Race to the Top Grants that were promised to the states by the Federal Government in 2010.

While a common core curriculum appears to make sense, if one wishes to achieve *minimal* proficiency levels in the younger generations, the approach has serious deficiencies.

The first and foremost objection is that the standards are copyrighted, meaning that the states cannot make changes that fit their particular needs. The second one is that there is no available evidence that the proposed curriculum is effective; in other words, rather than trying the curriculum in various localities first and determining its effectiveness, the educational authorities defend it on purely theoretical grounds, with the acknowledgement that it may be modified in the future. This is simply putting the cart before the horse.

The third objection is that the establishment of national standards, with the support of the federal government, appears to be a direct challenge to the US Constitution, which places education entirely in the hands of the states. The fourth one is equally incriminating because it is abundantly clear that input to the process was denied to a vast number of stakeholders, including local school boards, teachers' organizations, and parents; this is a damning fact in a democratic system of governance.

The fifth objection is that the support for the Common Core Curriculum by private foundations gives credibility to the charge that the educational standards favor the ideologies of organizations willing to accept tax-exempt status. The sixth one is that there is no reason to believe that different schools, geared to the various abilities of different students, should accept a standard curriculum. (Self-actualization, in fact, requires stratified standards.) Finally, although no state or national legislature can bind future legislatures to specific policies, the adoption of a national standard makes it difficult (but not impossible) to make changes that are agreeable to new legislative bodies at various local and state levels.

The formal establishment of standards in the educational sector is no different than the establishment of so-called national standards in the healthcare sector. While most people would agree that medical doctors should have medical degrees, there is no reason to think that those professional standards cannot be managed at the state level, as done in the past. Some poor states may feel a desperate need to improve their medical services and may adopt standards, for example, that allow foreign-trained doctors into their markets. The evidence demonstrates that even within individual states, hospitals follow different procedures, despite the fact that all doctors in that particular state passed the same set of exams.

It makes sense for the federal government to provide factual information about the differences within the states and among the states, and fight arduously for the disclosure of information about the outcomes that can be expected from various hospitals and schools. But that is quite different from arguing that the federal government should have a direct role to play in defining or implementing standards in either education or health care.

It is ironic that the federal government fights forcefully all inquiries about its managerial decisions, while at the same time trying to establish uniform standards for everyone else and demanding transparency from others. We still do not know what happened in Benghazi, Libya or who was responsible for the sale of guns to Mexican criminals in the Fast and Furious scandal, or who is responsible for the debacle in setting up the national healthcare website. And to compound matters, we have a Freedom of Information Act supposedly allowing citizens on the outside to obtain information, but only at a great cost to them.

Nowhere has secrecy in government been better demonstrated than in the NSA scandal, revealed by the low-level employee Edward J. Snowden. Not only was the National Security Agency listening to Americans' communications, but the agency was listening in on foreign leaders and "friends." It is now quite clear that the agency can disseminate the information it gets to police authorities; but these, in turn, cannot use the information in courts of law because it would be inadmissible. Local authorities need to find alternative sources for the information that they already have!

On July 31st, 2014 the CIA admitted breaking into the electronic records of a Congressional Committee, and yet no one was fired at the CIA.[6] The press, in turn, failed to ask a crucial question about the Snowden debacle; namely, if this was the most important intelligence failure over the past fifty years, isn't the Administration in charge responsible and accountable for this failure? The lack of accountability in government (regardless of the political party in control) is the best indicator that the people have ceased to have power over government officials.

We live in an age where the failures of the big financial institutions are taken in stride, with no one made responsible for them. These failures originated, in large part, when financial institutions were forced to make loans to individuals with poor credit ratings. This development took place as a result of the Community Reinvestment Act (CRA) of 1972. Most people are unaware of the consequences of this legislation. From 1977 to 1992, a total of $43 billion were loaned out as a result of this act; but when President Clinton took office, lending began to rise quite rapidly. By the year 2000, banks were committing $1.3 trillion of loans per year for questionable projects, and the yearly amount rose to $4.6 trillion in the last year of the Bush presidency! These loans were made with the assistance of activist organizations, such as ACORN, the New Jersey Citizens Action and the California Reinvestment

Coalition—each of which got commitments from banks totaling $760 million, $8 billion and $70 billion respectively from private banks. By the year 2007, activist groups had obtained bank commitments for questionable loans amounting to $867 billion. Not only that, but these activist organizations obtained direct fees in the millions of dollars for helping to administer the directed credit programs.[7] The educational failures of public school systems are blamed on previous educational policies, but no one is made responsible for those. There are catastrophic incidents where large corporations or wealthy individuals have to pay big settlements, yet the courts seal the agreements and hide the payments made. Courts also seal findings on foreclosures, seizure of property, the reputation of individuals, etc. Who is it that wins and who is it that loses in these court cases?

Secrecy is by far the most effective means of state control. If someone else knows what you are doing, and you are unaware of this, you can be defeated in achieving the goals that you set for yourself: that is what covert intelligence is all about. If someone else needs your cooperation, he or she can either blackmail you or else present you with an interpretation of the issues that fit your biases and preference, regardless of the true state of affairs. Governments love foreign leaders who can be manipulated, whenever governments are aware of those leaders' personal secrets.

When legislators work in secret, or when legislation "needs" to be passed in the middle of the night before the public finds out what it really means (as epitomized by former Speaker of the House Nancy Pelosi, who famously declared regarding Obamacare, "You need to pass it in order to find out what's in it"), the political process breaks down and everyone is in for extremely unpleasant surprises.

Also, the intelligence services need by necessity to work in secret, and their work is very difficult to evaluate. But there is no doubt that either the incompetence of the intelligence services, or possibly the deceit by President George W. Bush, led to the failure to inform Congress of the true situation in Iraq with regard to weapons of mass destruction, giving rise to a disastrous intervention in that country.

The situation can be worse if you know that someone in government knows exactly what you are doing! This is the technique used in totalitarian regimes, which we do not face in this country. In Cuba, for instance, practically everyone has to engage in robbery to survive the dire economic situation—yet the government is fully informed and does nothing . . . until its officials decide that the citizens have stepped too far beyond what the government tolerates. That is a regime of fear.

In America, a somewhat similar situation arises when the government engages in a tax audit, for the law is so complicated that you can always be put through the ringer, unless you have the money to challenge the government lawyers. The IRS scandals during the Nixon and Obama administrations are chilling examples of what is becoming a trend in government agendas: the greater control of citizens.

Hence good government, from the point of view of government officials, is one that offers cheap bread and a lot of circuses, absolves school officials and business leaders from failed policies, prevents the press and the Congress from discovering the facts about political scandals, manipulates the opposition by means of information control, keeps the public in fear of IRS audits, and allows the courts to keep under wraps the monetary consequences of their decisions.

If the reader accepts most, if not all, of the arguments that we have put forward so far, two questions need to be answered.

First, what are the moral foundations that will lead people to challenge the elites and behave in a different way? People seem to care only about their personal happiness, while allowing the civic structure of society to fall apart. In other words, how can we convince people that personal happiness should not be their supreme goal—for it is that goal which is undermining our national institutions. America is a happy place where people are enjoying vicarious lives: those of their heroes in the sports, musical and theatrical arenas. Leaders in the public and private sectors face no consequences for their misguided policies. Neither the press nor the Congress discharges its responsibilities as a watchdog. Even politics is becoming a reality show!

It is not surprising, then, that education in America is becoming a farce, for few care to acquire the learning and skills that will make them fulfill their own potential. We are surviving on borrowed time, as we import from abroad the technicians and scholars that we so desperately need in an advanced economy.

Second, what rules need to be implemented to create an environment that is more liberating to the average person? The answer is complicated. We will argue that cheap bread is quite desirable, as long as people have to pay for it out of their own pocket-—for the simple reason that such course of action requires people to improve their skills. Otherwise, we create a culture of dependency and grow ever more entitlements for more dependents. The circuses have to be avoided through personal awareness of their existence, the understanding of their workings, and a felt repugnance for their consequences; it is easy, far too easy, to enjoy the circuses (and the infinite variety of gimmicks provided by the not-so-social media) and take them for granted as part of our culture. We should try to prevent subsidized circuses, no matter how much we personally enjoy them.

Educational and business leaders must face consequences when their schools do not perform well and when their businesses fail to follow legal standards. School officials need to be fired when their schools fail to perform at predetermined levels. The leniency of the courts towards financial fraud is amazing, penalizing the owners of the businesses rather than their directors with jail time.

Avoiding secrecy would seem the easiest issue to handle; yet that requires our active participation in the political process, which is intrinsically prone to secrecy. The key to defeating the purveyors of secrecy is the realization that those who support secrecy in government are those who can be bought. Hence we need policies that must abolish institutional arrangements that give rise to the likelihood that someone or some organization might be bought. What does that mean? For starters, all nonprofits, receiving preferential tax treatment, must be treated as for profit institutions. Most everyone receiving preferential tax treatment is unwilling to challenge government and, in principle, could be bought. (We make an exception for religious organizations because their leaders are supposed to have exemplary morals, but that exception must be narrowly drawn and defined.) Taxes, of course, must be as uniform as humanly possible, with no exceptions granted. The poor must even contribute to the common good, by engaging in community services.

And a lot more should be done, but we need to understand first how all of the above has come to pass, and that is the topic of the next few chapters.

NOTES

1. To verify this claim, readers can search YouTube to view historical documentaries on the "Circus Maximus" and the so-called "Seven Wonders of Ancient Rome." We will make many references to Greece and Rome, and we urge readers unfamiliar with these countries and their empires to look up their histories in encyclopedias available in the Internet. These tend to be reliable sources written by scholars for the general public. Make sure that the articles are signed and someone takes responsibility for their content.

2. The information on population is available in the monthly estimates of the United States Population, US Census Bureau for 1983 and 2014. Information on the Food Stamp Program and the Price indices needed to make the calculations in the text can be accessed in the *Statistical Abstract of the United States*, for various years. These sources are available in the Internet, but we urge the readers to get a hold of hard copies of government documents to get a good feel of how the data is compiled and contrasted over the years. Most local libraries, and of course all college libraries, will have copies of the *Statistical Abstract of the United States*. Note that the Food Stamp Program was renamed the Supplemental Nutrition Assistance Program (SNAP) in 2008.

3. There is a vast amount of literature on this subject. A classic study on this issue is the article by Robert A. Baade, Robert Baumann and Victor Matheson, "Selling the Game: Estimating the Economic Impact of Professional Sports through Taxable Sales," *Southern Economic Journal* 74, no. 3 (2008):794–810. A broader argument than the one made in the text, which includes sports as one of several possible cultural events, is made by Sang Mi Park, "The Paradox of Postcolonial Korean Nationalism: State-Sponsored Cultural Policy in South Korea, 1965–Present," *The Journal of Korean Studies* 15, no. 1 (2010): 67–93.

4. Many short but accurate articles can be found on the Internet, but we warn the readers for a second time to make sure that someone takes responsibility for them. A brief history of the antitrust exemption is Peter Bendix, "A History of Baseball's Antitrust Exemption," last updated December 3, 2008 and accessed October 30, 2015, http://www.beyondtheboxscore.com/2008/12/3/678134/the-history-of-baseball-s. A huge number of articles appear in the mainstream press, such as the *Wall Street Journal*; see Brent Kendall, "Supreme Court on Deck in

MLB Antitrust Battle?" Last updated January 15, 2015, accessed October 30, 2015, http://www.wsj.com/articles/baseballs-antitrust-exemption-upheld-in-appeals-court-1421347744.

5. Again, the *Statistical Abstract of the United States* is the best source for all these numbers.

6. This was widely reported in the American press and television, and that is why we do not provide any specific source. We assume that readers have their own preferred news sources, and they can look them up without our own interference.

7. All of these activities are fully documented in the book by Charles W. Calomiris and Stephen H. Haber, *Fragile by Design* (Princeton University Press, 2014): 216–226.

Chapter Three

The Philosophical Case
for Limiting Government

Which functions do governments discharge that are both intrinsic to them (no one else can do the same) and legitimate (no other entity should be given the right to do the same)? If some functions of public service can and must be discharged for the common good through executive power, legislative action, or decisions of the judiciary, how is the government's sovereignty over individuals defined and directed to its proper goal?

Certain functions of government are intrinsic to civil and public society, while others are extrinsic to it by being useful or instrumental to those individuals acquiring certain private goods. The functions that are intrinsic and necessary are: Justice, defense, and the regulation of commerce (which establishes the rules of the game, not the direction or goals of trade)—in addition to providing for the truly needy. Such functions deliver assistance to any individual against harm from others or defective communication; they guarantee any and all of the citizens' natural rights when they interact with their peers—these rights reaffirm and guarantee liberty, equal treatment and civil independence. A group of peers, it is rightfully assumed, would always be partial, either because of their limited understanding of the matters involved and of their particular interests. Hence a neutral, more informed and professional class of civil servants is brought in to facilitate those transactions intrinsic to the functions of the government.

But there are other functions and transactions that are extrinsic to government as such, while being potentially instrumental in the lives of individuals: education, health, and financial services. These functions assist the particular individual in reaching his or her own goals and can never be put on the same footing as justice, defense and the regulation of commerce (whose benefits are certifiably universal). Although freedom of access must be guaranteed as

19

a matter of principle, the eventual outcome is always a matter of luck and personal effort; which means that governmental power is not the sole purveyor of the good life.

Equality of outcome is never achievable, nor is it what the individual seeks when attempting to make a difference in his or her life. Legislation, executive action, and judicial decisions may facilitate individual choice and outcome, as in the case of providing a basic support to those handicapped individuals or older citizens who are unable to fend for themselves. Yet we observe that some individuals accept the opportunity and the challenge to improve their circumstances while others take no such interest; some pursue goals and dreams while others make no go of it. The allocation of a better access to opportunity is what distributive justice works for, as Immanuel Kant pointed out, which is also premised on the three fundamental goals of public right: Liberty, equality of access, and civil independence (*Metaphysics of Morals*, first part, Doctrine of Right, paragraph 46). Let us accept these goals as our own.

Yet, with health, education and social services, politicians and the bureaucratic class facilitate ever-new forms of assistance—thereby being no-longer neutral in delivering the universal access opened up by distributive justice. Politicians and bureaucrats are weighing in on various aspects of "social" life, and the effect of this intrusion is reversing the three Kantian goals, thereby initiating the creation of dependency. Citizens do often notice that the involvement in the private lives of individuals by politicians and bureaucrats is directly self-serving.

Thus our question about the limits of government's involvement leads to another one, "Who knows best?" for someone. Will it be the individual with a real and existential stake in his decisions? Or will it be the bureaucratic facilitator assisting the beneficiary of a claim? Renewing the tradition of limited of government can only happen if citizens understand that (a) government is serviceable when precise attributions to its operations are made and (b) distributive justice (providing access to some for a reason, while implicitly not extending the same hand to others) is legitimate only depending upon certifiable conditions—with liberty and equality being enhanced while civil dependency is being avoided.

Defining government means that we start from "We the People" as the source of legislative power that binds all citizens in the future. Specific types of operations are then defined for, and restricted to, the executive power (the Government from its first officer down). Other operations of applicability of laws are assigned exclusively to judicial officers adjudicating cases (thereby assessing current laws) in various predefined courts. Hence, constitutional government is defined by functions and restrictions—an essential feature that was articulated by the Greek advocates of pluralism, especially Aristotle, and also by members of the Roman Republic. John Locke also brought this fundamental concern of limited government back to attention. And we all know that the American Founding Fathers made functions and restrictions the central piece of the work of the Convention giving us the American Constitution. Immanuel Kant restated similar criteria at about the same time.

Failing this structure of functional government and the discharging of its separate functions, power will be tyrannical and despotic, illegitimate though vested with the instruments of force and violence. Since individuals in positions of power tend to overlook, mishandle, pay little heed to the particulars of those they are supposed to benefit, power in the State is a delicate instrument—hence to be granted on special conditions. The reason is that this instrument can be at times sharp, cutting its way through a jungle of conflicting individual activities; at other times, it can be blunt, ineffective and illegitimate. The major problem for us assessing government is: How do we solidify legitimate government? And how do we mitigate or prevent the rise of bluntness, political ineffectiveness and illegitimacy?

Let's make a start through our use of common sense and our intuition of instrumentality and efficiency. We begin with matters economic by recognizing that all other aspects of life—personal, cultural, political, religious too—depend on what funds are there, what assets and revenue are available to discharge a given function. Good government is limited only because wealth (created only by individuals working together toward the concrete benefits that accrue to them) is properly allocated according to pre-agreed upon rules of the game.

Contracts specify which services are traded, for money or in-kind. In a free market no one is granted special treatment, no one favored and no one excluded. Equality under the law can only happen politically because, at a primary level, individuals are economic agents unobstructed by government. The favoritism of others is always correctly viewed as detrimental to yourself—and thus each person naturally understands they have a natural right not to be targeted for exclusion by their peers, and to them it means not to lose opportunities that serve other people's interests.

Political freedom and economic freedom are but the two sides of the same coin, where people take upon themselves to restrain the sovereign power of the state in order to retain and make permanent the benefits of public, universal, natural rights—not the privileges or specific rights secured for one individual or another. The act of enshrining a natural right into a constitutional guarantee, and the subsequent language of related bills makes such rights definitive or, in the language of Kant, peremptory and "conclusive" (*Metaphysics of Morals*, first part, Doctrine of Right, paragraph 15).

Are the two ideas of political freedom and economic freedom connected in the Western tradition? We see that they are. In the case of the ancient world of the Greeks (the free polis) and the Roman Republic, only individuals with property or group standing were allowed to participate. Economic independence gave to some individuals the leisure and the additional where-withal to take part in political matters—justice, war, and legislation. Because economic independence was a prerequisite for political franchise, and because the ancient households had slaves, political freedom could mean granting status and privilege to some, withholding the same from others assessed as "unequal" (a view that today we find unacceptable).

The most striking formulae came to us from Aristotle. Living in 4th century B.C. Athens, he originated in the state called Macedon. In his *Politics* he surveyed the essential information about all Greek states and the practices of the other cultures, Egyptian, Persian, etc. The fishbowl experiment of Greece—small landmass, extremely indented coastline, mountain separations—yielded trade and freedom of movement, and such useful things as writing and sharing great poetry, critical understanding of cultural differences, appreciation for the sciences, the benefits of economic development in small enclaves, and political reforms that restrained the power of the old elites and promoted the self-reliance of the democratic spirit of the middle class.

For Aristotle, his goal was to spell out the freedoms of the Greek city-states: Equality of all having franchise for access to these particular goods was the chief good—both descriptively and prescriptively. Laws can and should be so well crafted that equality under them (for the free citizens then, for all citizens now) will promote a unique way of life and mastery over one's future. Freedom cannot be defined by one type of man, one type of plan or ideas; freedom always borrows from clues and warnings from different individuals and different groups, different trades and different ways of life, different opinions and different appreciations of things. Let only one man, idea, lifestyle, or opinion be given absolute power and sway, and the good life is over.

These three sets of descriptions (and prescriptions) account for political plurality; a failure to follow them will yield corruption and decay:

1. There can be one man or woman at the top of the political society, a structure then called "monarchy." This person follows precedents and consults the people before acting. The king's or queen's power to affect the lives of others is not absolute and cannot be thought so superior and infallible that he or she can dispense with the assessments and opinions of others in the realm. The Greek tragedies written and produced by the famous playwrights repeat the point: Should the person at the top fail to hear out all the people involved, his or her rule no longer follows best advice, his or her own ego bloated with hubris gets in the way, the regime is then "tyranny" and the man or woman a "tyrant."

2. There can be several individuals at the top, a structure called "aristocracy." Honors go to specific individuals and their families, each one led by obligations of service. Privileges are enshrined in traditions of public service. Because of these contributions to public service and spending, the aristocratic system may continue to propagate itself. A connection and fusion with monarchy can occur. Yet that very system can also veer into a rule of a protected rich and superior class, who would then create laws to prevent the rise of newcomers and inhibit the decline of inept individuals from their ranks. The corruption of aristocracy is called "oligarchy," the rule of the wealthy and well connected, ruling for themselves to the detriment of all others is called "plutocracy."

3. There can also be a political structure premised under the emergence of individuals irrespective of class considerations. This is "democracy," in which power is granted to all on account of the need for "fairness" to enable the rise of talent or ideas. All free citizens are invited, and expected, to participate. All are needed to understand laws and decisions, to defend themselves in private matters and take part in public service. Socrates was an example of that ability of an Athenian man to figure out what is good or bad practice for someone or for the city, good or bad opinion, good or bad policy—and why. Yet this very system involves hard work, and when insurmountable tensions arise and consensus fails, power veers into in the hands of interest groups or strong individuals (the "demagogues") who manipulate the many, excite them through fear-mongering and anger, and distort facts and issues. There is, then, a corruption of the system of "democracy" which is "mob rule" to the benefit of a tyrant with connections to trusted oligarchs.

Summarizing Aristotle's account, we have three positive, effective forms of government, none of which is exclusive of the others: monarchy, aristocracy, democracy; and three corrupt governments, each one unstable and likely to slip into the next one: tyranny, oligarchy, and mob-rule. What makes good government "good" are individuals, with character, morals, careful thinking (prudence) and the ability to make decisions that reflect respect for self and consideration for others, capable of stepping forth with courage, always on the lookout for justice, and capable of self-control. Those virtues—prudence, justice, courage, self-control—enable the active citizen to become wise in practical matters, and this wisdom ends up reflected in government. These virtues are self-limiting (as focusing on the right action) and they also reflect on good government.

What makes the bad government "bad" are individuals with unchecked character flaws, no predictable habits of excellence, and a tendency to obfuscate others. They view their neighbors as pawns or enemies. They resort to preferential treatment in laws and edicts, they display the arrogance of superiority, they are a law unto themselves, preempt debates and forsake trust and mutual confidence. Equality for the few, inequality for the many—such are the corrupt laws where some are more equal than others, where the law divides to enshrine privileges and never unites to give an opportunity to new enterprise and talent. The typical birds of a feather are: the demagogues, the oligarchs, and the fools who sing their praise and use their own freedom in denying that of others. Unchecked egos reflect corrupt practices—at that point good government, which is energetic yet limited, is forsaken.

As we all know, the history of freedom in Greece did not last very long and the constitutional government in place among the Romans also fell in decline when the Empire replaced the Republic. In the Roman case, good and limited republican government collapsed under the pressure of the Republic unleashing wars of conquest and domination, then having to control and maintain sovereignty over the many lands and peoples that it had conquered. Good emperors succeeded bad ones, and vice versa. The model of the Roman imperial state was not citizens keeping government limited and checked through an ethics of discipline, self-control and thoughtful interaction. Instead, the lead of the state was provided by a Caesar, the sovereign reasserting the prerogatives of a master with a rubber-stamp Senate. Such attributes allowed warriors and State officials to manage and control all parts of the Empire, in the attempt to keep them all at peace while also sharing the spoils of war and the tributes of *pax romana* with an elite class.

Two things profoundly changed the Empire and ultimately destroyed it: (1) "Give to Caesar what is Caesar's, and give to God what is God's" and (2) the Germanic invasions causing the Empire to split, sending its capital to Constantinople. In other words, first, there was Christianity and its message, or good tidings, that each individual is unique—to be acknowledged with respect, love and charity. Second, there was the message of surprise and novelty, delivered by the Germanic invasions of peoples not previously known as entities and now pushing to establish their control beyond their own economically backwards parts of Europe. These two separate but also historically connected forces dismantled the remnants of the Empire. They also suggested to men that the ultimate higher attribute of perfect justice only belonged to God and—lo and behold—couldn't be fathomed, although it should be aspired to and respected by men. Meanwhile, on earth, the fall of that Empire meant that men could and should live moral lives, taking care of themselves, unmolested by their fellows.

Everyone knows, of course, that this idea was wishful thinking as long as feudal masters ruled over rural populations in Europe; and the East was in the grips of various religious feuds, the most serious emanating from the Muslim expansion. That expansion moved to the Western part through Spain where it stopped, while continuing to exert pressure upon the eastern part of Europe until the decisive naval defeat of the Muslims at Lepanto in 1571. Such a check on Muslim imperial expansion was reiterated at Vienna, at the battle of September 12, 1683.

Renewed communication and freedom from invasion caused the idea of limited government to return to the Western Mediterranean and the Northern parts of Europe. The decisive element now was competition and the ability to innovate, which only the middle class would bring to unexpected heights. Their lifestyle of comfort, innovation and accomplishments depended upon property rights and led to capital accumulation through commerce and trade—also merging the old work ethic with the idea of a service to all, not service to one or a few.[1]

Europe changed the world because the idea of limited government started to percolate. No longer were the King and the Peers, the Emperor and the Princes, the Sovereign and Suzerains alone in determining the rules of the game. The idea of limited government became more congenial to the English, whose aristocracy reasserted the need for a charter, and whose middle class rejected the monopoly of religion and foreign dictates upon the state, re-establishing the principle of "Give to Caesar what is Caesar's, and to God what is God's." Only then, was it clear that modern day sovereigns and landlords were to be constrained by the wishes of their people, especially the "middling" class, or Middle Class.

The English historian Lord Acton shows that the fight for freedom in Europe was waged by this new innovative class appealing to a proper understanding of religion, charity and tolerance (thus to the priests and educators) against the privileges of the Hidalgos and Entitled Landlords of various titles. It was the bourgeoisie who reintroduced freedom to the Western European world, in terms both of economics and of politics, the two being inescapably intertwined.[2]

Although the origins of legitimate government came from granting and limiting powers of individuals and groups—as pointed out by Aristotle in describing constitutional government against its corruptions—the modern point was made that a universal idea of the natural rights of all individuals preceded all transactions, private and public, and provided a blueprint for what the common good would never exclude. Natural rights are fundamental rights of non-interference. They merely put me in charge of what is already mine and they put you in charge of what is already yours. Hence, these rights need validation, the crafting of a constitution preventing liberties from being crushed by the liberty of others or the tyranny of some. This was the task taken up by the American Founding Fathers.

For Kant, at the same time, this meant that some essential supplement had to be provided to the natural rights theory. Kant describes and prescribes their reality being acknowledged publicly and politically as giving them a "conclusive" (or peremptory and authoritative) status. In constitutional devices and legal contraptions, the prevention or punishment of abuse must be articulated. Mechanisms for public "tranquility" and redress are sine-qua-non conditions of civil society. In a concrete way these mechanisms secure the rights of persons against any peer, or a group of peers that is happy to trample upon the first. They serve as the original principles allowing access to opportunities for all, allowing people freedom on how they want to live and be of service to others—and on how they will maintain their independence unmolested by outside interference.

This promotion of natural rights becoming conclusive and guaranteed in constitutional law only came to be when men and women could think beyond limited horizons, when land and real estate were no longer the main source of wealth through serf labor. Various engines of freedom had come together: the Muslim defeat at Lepanto, Galileo, and the emerging middle class. In the lives of individuals this meant that services—labor, work, and the various performances of doctors, lawyers, teachers, actors, and inventors—played an increasing public role in the new society, a role that inevitably diminished the prestige of the grandees.

When the American Founding Fathers exerted their best minds on the meticulous crafting of the checks and balances of the Constitution, they knew that the inroads of money and inequality (the oligarchy and elitism of the well-connected) would need to be reformed periodically in the Republic. They sought periodic elections; they counted on diversity and clash of interests (in a large country) as the bulwark against the absolutism of control rampant in most of Europe.

To the Founding Fathers, it was royal absolutism and the Machiavellian war games played by royalty and the local aristocracies that were making civil life dispiriting on the European continent for the middle or lower classes. The Founding Fathers' and the immigrants' belief in democratic equality and disapproval of European power games is enshrined in the Whig (anti-Tory) principle of not accepting aristocratic titles in the new republic. The new republic guaranteed that all new participants were to be given an equal and fair chance at new opportunities. Their one weakness was the acceptance of slavery as a political compromise; this error led to the Civil War seventy years later.

American founders were helped at first by America's relative strength in defending new territories, and their ability to stand apart from European power games, with the Monroe Doctrine becoming an integral part of America's unwillingness to share in European contests. And when the European nation states spread their modern global imperial fleets—replete with bureaucracies, industrial investors and adventurers—America embarked into an era of industrial development, the so-called "Gilded Age." This led to the unprecedented economic development in North America—but it kept unresolved the failure of Reconstruction and it finally allowed for the gradual domination of national life by the special interests, when it came to dealing with the outside world. When the so-called Roosevelt Corollary to the Monroe Doctrine was adopted, this changed the meaning given to it by its author, John Quincy Adams. And so it came to pass that when European imperialism was spreading its wings on a global scale, America didn't resist government's growth and her progressive presidents (Theodore Roosevelt and Woodrow Wilson) pushed for foreign outreach or intervention.

The obliteration of liberty, equality and civil independence in colonial societies, and even at home in America (where the Great War could not even be criticized), took on global proportions because Western capitalists called on their governments to assist them in their gambling investments in foreign lands; these included Panama, Mexico and Cuba in the Americas and large segments of the Muslim world and Sub-Saharan Africa. Meanwhile, Western home markets were restricted by tariffs and national protectionism. Corporate welfare was thus born or expanded in the granting of entitlements and privileges to special interest groups.

To reaffirm the dignity of man against the indignities visited by government powers, today's citizens need to dismantle rules that restrict freedom of exchange in goods, services and ideas; and they must have the freedom to attempt local solutions to problems that have a local origin. The proper functions of governments are and can only be justice, defense and the regulation of commerce—in addition to providing for the truly needy. Governments may facilitate but must not discharge other social functions—if they do, they will deprive individuals of a basic ethics of responsibility and force them into collusion with crony capitalism and bureaucratic socialism.

Only individuals should carry out the control and encouragement of proper government. This control can only come from the informed citizenry who pay taxes and live with the outcome of public actions funded by their taxes. Empowering a universal middle class to act in the interest of all and preventing legal favoritism means more prosperity for all to enjoy, more services to the less advantaged, and more freedom for others to come. Such is the real meaning of distributive justice: Limiting government sovereignty and returning power and money to people intent on results rather than securing privileges—such is the goal of an ethics of responsibility, which is our next topic of discussion.

Before we proceed, it is worth repeating the fundamental principles that serve to align values and politics are liberty, equality of access and civil independence. While wars can and should be undertaken as a defense of these principles, as was done in the Second World War, most wars are destructive of those principles, both at home and abroad. We will address the role of the government towards the truly needy in Chapter 9.

NOTES

1. The emergence of a non-zero-sum gain was decisive in evolving crafts and encouraging risk-taking, which greatly augmented the wellbeing of individuals and populations. The history of this discovery made possible the increased interaction and cultural connections between the populations and educated trading partners. Pluralism is the precondition for, as well as the result of, this unfolding and can only function within a system of limited government. See Robert Wright, *Nonzero, The Logic of Human Destiny* (New York: Vintage Book, 2001).

2. In a wording very similar to Kant's view, Lord Acton defines liberty not in terms of permissiveness but instead of our caring for others—which includes the limiting of the permissiveness of the others and governments: "Liberty is not the power of doing what we like, but the right of being able to do what we ought." See Jordan J. Ballor, "Lord Acton on Catholic and Modern Views of Liberty," last revised on July 17, 2013, accessed October 19, 2015, http://blog.acton.org/archives/57615-lord-acton-on-catholic-and-modern-views-of-liberty.html.

Chapter Four

Caring for Others
Requires a Principle of Duty

The topic of this difficult chapter aims at answering the question, "Is morality à la Carte?" Is the menu revisited periodically to be appealing to the customer? Or is morality something that neither the crowd nor we can change or adapt to the taste of the day? Is morality an affair that goes over and beyond our average daily choices, our average way of reasoning about events and people? Is something lost when morality is made relative to people and circumstances, when excuses are made to fit certain events rather than rationales and principles held before acting?

Our starting point is the following observation: What people care for is seen, typically, as what they like personally and/ or what they value personally. So we ask the question, can there be a difference between what people like and value personally and the principles of a morality valid for all? Whenever not prevented by circumstances stemming from other individuals, from the world or from a lack of true insight, *people do what they want*. Their preferences and their values are part of a "personal" package: you get the person, and you get some baggage with him or her. From a psychological assessment of conduct or behavior, short of addictions, people will strike the outside observer as willful to various degrees. They pursue things with more or less tenacity; we see they can sometimes be persuaded to do something different. Yet sometimes they cannot and will not budge, and the person trying to change that behavior hits on a wall of stubbornness. Whatever the level of their fastidiousness, obstinacy or flimsiness, it can be argued by outside observers that such people at a given time always do what they want most. So the criterion of "willing" seems never absent, nor is it irrelevant, in the descriptions and pronouncements of an outsider observer on someone's life.

But is this the right, or correct, assessment of what goes on in moral life? In other words, is the value of morality (and understanding what we care for) something graspable from the outside as an act of willing, and open to various grades of preference? Or alternatively, is the value of morality and understanding what we care for . . . *something greater than ourselves*, something that can and should be expressed only from a universal perspective, where the rationale for willing something "moral" originates?

In other words, should we look at morality from the vaunted individual perspective or should we approach it from the universal perspective of rational persons determining that there are things and principles of supreme importance to them as moral persons? Typically, the act of thinking involves such criteria as the Golden Rule or the directive that "punishment ought to fit the crime." For it seems that if we fail to take this approach, morality and values would slip into preferences of taste about which no definitive rational conclusion can ever be made (we don't argue about tastes!) and in which change can happen anytime.

Immanuel Kant puts us on the way to consider that the morality we care for as rational beings is more than the ability to pronounce an opinion on something like . . . eating with forks, spoons, knives, chopsticks, or our fingers, as opposed to with knitting needles and tweezers. To be sure, some people may for a while choose knitting needles and tweezers as utensils for eating if a majority have already stated their "preference" for forks, spoons, knives, chopsticks and fingers over anything else. Certain individuals, we observe, may be definite contrarians, perhaps because cultures, taken individually and in the aggregate, may be seen also as contrarian to other cultures in matters of tastes or preferences. Everyone knows that slurping is frowned upon in most Western countries, while it is a sign of appreciation of food in several Eastern ones. An infinite number of similar instances of cultural diversity can be given here. The whole point is that many things, in such matters of taste, are done for or with a purpose, as opposed to randomly.

Kant defines the will ("the faculty of desire"[1]) as the ability to cause things to exist and occur in the world simply because we thought of them in advance and then sought to implement what we represented beforehand. The ability to represent on the basis of what we know, like and dislike, tolerate or do not tolerate, find or do not find acceptable/desirable, and then to act on this representation—this is the will. The only alternative to willing is an act prompted by instinct, as in the case of animal behavior or automatic reflex. There are innate values in what animals do and what automatic reflex actions achieve, for example the migration of birds, their mating rituals, or in the case of humans the ability to walk upright and to recapture your balance when threatened to lose it. None of these "actions" entail the ability to choose, and they are connected to the preservation of life for the individual or the species. They are not directly connected with representation.

The question then arises, what are the actions *only humans can perform* because there is a rational choice involved? The need for certain unusual actions and a new direction originates in the individual human predicament of being lost, or being "at an end," which only our thinking detects in its gravity and from which rescue can only come in thought-out analysis first and foremost.[2] *What ought I to do?* My first hope is that someone may come, or agree to come, to my rescue and be willing to tell me what to do, because they either have the experience and a solution to my predicament. But being at an end reasserts itself. What if this person fails to show up or somehow makes a mistake. So while I may presuppose that certain people have my interest at heart or in mind, there is too much uncertainty and doubt, and in the end I must resort to thinking on my own, "What should my goal be?" and "What end should I pursue?"

We become aware of good, bad and evil when we have to take care of ourselves—and when this responsibility impacts others, who happen to be free too! Such is the warning clearly issued to us by our parents and educators when they want us to face the world responsibly. They encourage us to rely on ourselves rather than on faith in the smooth talkers. This situation is in fact the "natural" one for Kant. For in the state of nature, we originate in circumstances of poverty, scarcity and inability to communicate essential aspirations. In that state of nature our latent moral aspirations of liberty, equality of access and civil independence are almost always systematically trumped by other circumstance, including the most pressing need, urge, passion or desire expressed by many individuals around us. This situation will inevitably generate either perplexity or anxiety. But the flip side of the conundrum is that we are now fully invested with the ability to think rationally in order to take stock of wrongs and evils, but also to make our way into adulthood (or civilization) after taking leave of our state of early innocence (or barbarism).

Our parents and educators, of course, are quite aware of the unfortunate status of their offspring and wards. They want to mitigate it as soon as possible, and so they nudge us into using our "faculties" and they urge us to "grow up" and recognize how to deal with things. We no sooner emerge from the paradise of being cared for in our childhood than we are forced, coerced, cajoled into having to think for ourselves. We go to school, we are presented with role models, we are given "tools" for success, and yet not too much assistance is forthcoming on how to think on our own. It seems that these tools and role models put us on the way to thinking on our own, but still broader questions loom.

Isn't the state of dependency and innocence—according to Kant our original condition and one we must overcome—something requiring more than instruments? Don't we need a constant orientation to a community of agents, respecting each other's freedom as a matter of principle, thinking in agreement before they—and we with them—strike out on our own? Although we are aware that each one being successful may change his or her life for the better, a bigger idea emerges that only in thinking of myself as another, and of others as myself, can I change the world.

Kant argues that a universally valid morality[3] enables us to stand and think beyond the ordinary considerations that matter to human beings. Our moral being is rooted in our willingness to choose an act that is far more important and difficult than managing average or everyday dealings with things and people. It is also rooted in the awareness that humans have a will that is capable of good and evil.

In those everyday dealings with things and people, we understand a goal, analyze how it can be met, and we contemplate the principle and the means for reaching the goal. We follow instrumental, extrinsic connections (between events) as they are in the world. It takes some research and also calls for some practice. We make ourselves instrumental in obtaining benefits of various kinds. Over and beyond these instrumental connections, morality stands and makes us think of the special attention we have to pay to certain things. Not-killing, not-lying, not-ignoring others—hence making sure we go out of our way to protect others, speak the truth to them, and acknowledge them—these are not acts showing an instrumental and extrinsic good, they are acts with internal and intrinsic goodness in themselves. They are not conditioned upon a prior emotion—fear of something or desire for a pleasurable benefit—they are caused by a good will that discounts the fear or the possible benefit. This will put the value upon the act itself.

But we also see that we, or others, at times could do the opposite. So the freedom of our will is something we understand in connection with the possibility in willing and doing evil—through boldness and deception. Morality is caught between—standing over and beyond—pure instrumental thinking and the immorality of its internal assailants—the thief, the liar, and the criminal.

Morality is a matter of choice—of principles that can be universally recommended in the act you engage in. In the case of instrumental thinking, the morality of universally recommendable principles is not involved. Indeed, there is a choice of specific instruments and of the particular principles to follow. In the case of immorality (contravening to the Golden Rule), morality is clearly dismissed—involved and recognized at the outset, yet in the next step overcome and denied. We start to understand that the good will is good intrinsically, while the instrumental and external good of particular achievements may never be allowed to overstep their limited application.

When we become students of ethics, we start to understand that evil is the individual's potential to will a course of action that directly belies the universal recommendation of the Golden Rule. And we also come to realize that, of the evils of the world, some may be caused by misfortune while others are the outcome of devilish acts performed by immoral individuals, among whom we could include ourselves potentially or even actually. Following Kant, students of ethics seek to examine the principles of actions as they manifest themselves in an ethics of responsibility—applying to these principles the prevention of objective wrong ("The Doctrine of Right" is the first part of the *Metaphysics of Morals*) as well as being fleshed out in a fuller conception of ethics, with virtue and education being exposed to young wards ("The Doctrine of Virtue" is the second part of that same text).

Our task, right now[4], is to gain clarity on the principles of instrumental advancement, which we are prone to regard correctly as essential to moving from dependency on parents and traditions, into the greater independency of the individual thinking on his or her own. The principles of instrumental advancement are what Kant calls "hypothetical imperatives." Adopting a given hypothetical imperative means that we prefer something better over something worse; we internally turn to discipline and expertise and reject indolence and ignorance in order to achieve an external good. For ourselves following the hypothetical imperatives of cooking, building and taking care of ourselves, we see reasons why not to indulge certain options, we see the negatives of certain outcomes. There are options we reject only because there are other real things we contemplate and care to achieve. Such an elementary choice is presented, and remains present, to commonsensical, rational people who want good things (in the instrumental world) for themselves—exchanging service for service, deferring to the experts, depending upon them, and requiring the ability to choose in order to achieve satisfaction.

It is common sense and an act of instrumental reason to be grateful for a world in which individuals cared enough to become experts in their line of business and were free to do so. This is a world where "hypothetical imperatives" (as rules of skill) are recognized and emulated. The spread of knowledge and the ease of transactions (through travel and the ability to trade goods) are at the beginning of the Enlightenment, where we dare to know and think on our own. The rules of skill, which Kant identifies at the first level of the imperatives of practical reason, make a difference in the rational activity of humans, who unlike animals no longer live under the dominance of instinct and seek to overcome obstacles they can analyze and from which they can find relief.

The second level of hypothetical imperatives is what Kant calls "counsels of prudence." This is relevant to situations in one's professional as well as personal life. Counsels of prudence contain an infinite number of cases, all targeting general success in one's interactions with others. Kant presents these counsels as reasonable criteria with which an objective dispassionate observer or mentor will assist a friend or ward in need of advice. The characteristic of a counsel of prudence is that if you want happiness at the end, you will want the proper means to get there. And so there is what we may call logical connection between the end and the means, which the counselor or mentor's knowledge of the world offers.

This ability to connect variable but logical elements to help someone manage a professional or personal situation depends on the mentor's knowledge of the world and it depends on analyzing the situation properly. The connection between the solution and the means is instrumental and "analytic." If you want the end, you will seek the appropriate means.

So far—short of having clarified morality proper—students of ethics have only surmised the agent's willingness to choose a path to veer away from dangers and potential failure. This corresponds to what we described earlier as the human reality of "being at an end." And so far we surmised that the capacity to know and make the best decision lay with us, but the end was an instrumental good outside of us, for the sake of which we would select the proper means. We had to secure an appropriate connection between success and ourselves. To yield the best outcome, one has to undergo a test of discipline (in considering what works for securing those ends) and judicious thinking (in dealing with others).

By contrast now, students of ethics will see that caring for someone in an intrinsic way—whether the someone be you, your kin or your fellow—requires a different mode of thinking, and thus a different approach to principles of action. Telling the truth, making a promise that you keep, and acting benevolently without expecting a quid pro quo (i.e., being generous without advertising it)—these actions stand on their own. The good will of the person doing them recommends itself without further ado. *The action recommends the end in the end, not in the means.* The means of keeping the promise is to keep the promise. The means of telling the truth is telling the truth. And so on. Thus there is no search for the means, no search for wisdom or knowledge that would suddenly and finally come up in the search by a person wondering what to do. The person of good will won't have to ponder or go beyond the obvious. Conscience simply speaks: You've got to do what is good in an *intrinsic* way for you, your kin, or your fellow. And by the way, your kin and your fellows also know what is required of anybody to treat others in the right way.

We see that doing right always follows the Golden Rule—it is not a seeking the means appropriate to whatever end—*it is the affirmation of the end,* which freedom from the temptations to the contrary only establishes and reinforces. Established and reinforced freedom is a matter for thought and for being in the care of yourself without apprehensions of nagging of peers or of a displeased sovereign. Freedom is first and foremost connected to thinking, and thinking is first and foremost immediately connected to the assertion (the "categorical" assertion) that we care about ourselves, that we care about others, that we care that others not mistreat others, just like we refuse for ourselves any of the means by which somebody is treated as a pawn in somebody else's power game.

The categorical imperative is not an optional convention, to be dismissed or coldly manipulated by Machiavellians or the unrestrained, powerful individuals.[5] It is name of the real stakes for people freely endeavoring to live by rules that allow each to be equal, yet special, each time a person who communicates with others and with whom others care to communicate. This is the reason why morality always borrows from a cosmopolitan, in fact universal, legislation, "Act in such a way that the principle of your maxim (i.e., the intent in your decision) may become a universal law of nature."

We have now defined what lies at the center, and outside, of morality proper. We are in a much better position to answer the question about what cultural orientation and education will be advisable to a student of ethics, and what views on humankind will make a prescriptive ethics of responsibility. We take our bearings from Kant, again, but now from three different yet complementary perspectives: from his philosophy of right, from his philosophy of virtue, and from his ideas on taste.

We take another look at the "Doctrine on Right" because legal rights may limit our absolute freedom so that the natural rights of others are respected and stand in external compliance with the moral law. The fundamental interdictions of morality can be repeated and may be enforced with specific legal punishments. We start with natural rights of non-interference that will guarantee a "mine" and a "yours" not-to-be-stripped or altered by any intervention. This means that such rights are in fact inalienable and non-transferable.

These rights, first articulated by well-known luminaries of the Enlightenment, John Locke, Montesquieu, Adam Smith, need to be embraced and made "conclusive" (peremptory and authoritative (*Metaphysics of Morals*, "The Doctrine of Right," Section 15) in a binding constitution, which will make the civil bond of a people/nation dependent upon established institutions. Under such a constitution three guidelines are to be followed and pursued as ends: the liberty of the citizens under the law, their equality of access to the benefits provided in the public realm, and their civil independence.

This last criterion is essential for enabling the first two, as American Constitutionalists have always known. Threatening civil independence is the emergence of a progressively intrusive government, which started in the so-called "Reconstruction" of the South. The Civil Rights movement of the 20th century pushed against the nullification of the right to vote for Blacks (recalling that the Jim Crow laws were the anti-constitutional grand bargain of Reconstruction). The movement also pushed against the dependency on the erratic goodwill of others—in fact pushed against the predictable ill will of majorities of individuals in the Southern states. Only by asserting freedom through independence, and understanding of the promissory note of the Constitution, could Martin Luther King, Jr. and the Civil Rights guardians of the 1960s make clear to all the connection between the natural rights of all citizens and their independence from intrusive government—a connection that sounded the definitive end of segregation by constitutional means and reassertion of the U.S. Constitution as a document of intrinsic value, especially its preamble, the "Declaration of Independence."

Kant's philosophy of virtue also adds elements to our effort to flesh out an ethics of responsibility. Following this "Doctrine of Virtue" means that efforts will be made to encourage students and teachers to distinguish between so-called good intentions and a really effective goodwill. Tyrannies of the majority were anticipated by the American Founding Fathers, by Kant, de Tocqueville and many other writers in the age of democratic government. Since their warnings were issued, the various socialist revolutions have proven that the distinction between majority rule and rule of law was not moot. The road to hell is paved with "good intentions." Students of politics have to realize that all agents in the real world cannot agree on all things and that violence never creates, but only destroys, human plurality. Thus the mottos "the end justifies the means" (Machiavelli) or "might is right" (the Greek Sophists) should be analyzed, questioned and rejected. Both of these injunctions are in keeping with instrumental success, but they are inappropriate to an ethics of responsibility.

The same can be said of deceptions that destroy the common trust that fellow citizens build among themselves—forcing many into the realm of private concerns and the distrust of the public realm amidst growing cynicism. An ethics of responsibility[6] promotes discussion of role models, and exemplifies various types of decent, honest and truth-telling behaviors. Individual and their wards should also take stock of political, secular and religiously inspired role models from all cultures of the world.

The final element in fleshing out an ethics of responsibility is one dependent on taste. This is made possible thanks to private endowments and the cultural outreach of corporations and benefactors. Private citizens in their various communities offer grants and scholarship opportunities to broaden the perspectives of persons of all ages—the young as well as the old. Presenting great works of music, painting, theater or literature to audiences, and getting their feedback—their appreciation and critical assessments—are essential to the aesthetic judgment that Kant finds key for all to appreciate what is worthy of admiration in the world. Admiring is an essential trait of humans who are able to care for something greater than themselves—and this is also the hallmark of moral beings.

NOTES

1. See *The Metaphysics of Morals*, Section 2, "On the Relation of the Faculties of the Human Mind to Moral Laws": "The faculty of desire is the faculty to be, by means of one's representations the cause of the objects of these representations. The faculty of a being to act in accordance with representations is called life," 373. Also see *Critique of Judgment*, Section 1, "On the Division of Philosophy": "For the will, as the power of desire is one of the many natural causes in the world, namely the one that acts in accordance with concepts; and whatever we think of as possible (or necessary), as distinguished from the physical possibility or necessity of an effect whose cause is not determined to [exercise] its causality through concepts—but through mechanism, as in the case of lifeless matter or through instinct, as in the case of animals," 10.

2. Among the various impediments to thinking properly about our moral dimension and among the confusions humans may encounter or end up in, see Kant's accounts of our original temptation to give up the inquiry. In Section 1 of the *Groundwork of the Metaphysics of Morals,* one reads "We find that the more a cultivated reason purposefully occupies itself with the enjoyment of life and with happiness, so much the further does one get away from true satisfaction . . . They find that they have in fact only brought more trouble upon themselves instead of gaining in happiness. And because of this they finally envy rather than despise the more common run of people, who are closer to the mere natural instinct and do not allow their reason much influence on their behavior," 51.

3. This takes place, so to speak, in three installments, in the three essential texts by Immanuel Kant. All, including Kant, agree that the first and the third ones are more accessible than the second: (a) The *Grounding of the Metaphysics of Morals*; (b) *The Critique of Practical Reason*; and (c) *The Metaphysics of Morals*. It is also helpful to keep in mind Kant's essay called "Theory and Practice," see endnote 5 below.

4. We follow the main points of the *Grounding of the Metaphysics of Morals* (Sections 1 and 2).

5. See Kant's essay "Theory and Practice," whose Section 2 is pointedly directed "Against Hobbes." In it, Kant articulates the three a priori principles of (a) man's freedom as a human being, (b) man's equality as a subject, and (c) the independence of a member of the commonwealth as a citizen, and co-legislator; in *Kant: Political Writings*, ed. Hans Reiss, transl., H. B. Nisbet (Cambridge, UK: Cambridge University Press, 1991): 73–87.

6. We take the term from German sociologist Max Weber, but the development that we seek for it relies on the three characterizations of a human being endowed with freedom, equality and independence, and hence does not characterize a professional ethics, one reserved especially for civil servants. See Max Weber's "Politics as a Vocation" in *The Vocation Lectures*, trans. Rodney Livingstone (Indianapolis, IN: Hackett Publishing Company, 2004).

Chapter Five

Drawing the Line between Self-Actualization and Our Duty to Others

A mainstay of our arguments is that we stand for two generally compatible values, the first being self-actualization, and the second being a sense of duty towards others. We maintain that private property is a necessary condition for the achievement of self-actualization, since individuals need to acquire assets to achieve their full potential—which in no way means happiness. A person who has a special talent in musical composition, for example, achieves his or her self-actualization when he or she becomes a good composer; this achievement may require great personal sacrifice, since it could well involve ignoring other interests that the person has. Personal sacrifice to achieve self-actualization does not generally spawn happiness.

Some great composers, for example, found that they needed to live solitary lives and even give up marital relationships to concentrate fully on their goals; others did not, but even that did not mean that their spouses and children were sources of happiness—but rather sources of interruptions that required the assistance of others to overcome these distractions. This assistance, in turn, required the necessary income and assets to pay for it. Some other artists—like Walt Disney—required the control of vast assets to realize their dreams. In the case of Walt Disney, when viewed as an entrepreneur and entertainer, his self-actualization was intertwined with the creation of his vast enterprise.

We believe that no one would criticize a great composer and a great entrepreneur for their goals of self-actualization, since in both cases their goals served to improve or add to the lives of others. In effect, the performance of their duties towards others were embedded in their own self-actualization. However, this does not mean that such persons do not have to follow the Golden Rule; they must behave towards others the way they want others to behave towards them.

Regrettably, the acquisition of wealth and power is often detrimental towards acting in a moral way. It is part of the Golden Rule that people, all people, should be treated as ends and not as mere means. Therefore, if an entrepreneur like Disney behaved abusively towards the interests of his workers, then he deserved to be sued and restrained in his behavior—regardless of the potential impact of such a reprimand. There are no trade-offs involved when a great achievement is procured on the backs of people who are knowingly made to suffer. The Great Pyramids of Egypt should be both admired and despised (since they were built on the back of slaves); this perspective, we believe, is what makes our approach different and free of political biases.

This and subsequent chapters will address specific conflicts that exist between self-actualization and the duties that we have towards others; but we will also discuss possible means of overcoming these conflicts. The topic is difficult because the fallback position for many people is that income redistribution is the one and only action that needs to be taken in caring for others. This attitude is false. We pointed out in Chapter 2 (discussing bread and circuses) that few want to be interrupted from activities which bring them entertainment and pleasure, failing to realize that these activities neither bring about self-actualization nor satisfy the duties that they have towards others. While we will argue later in the book that there are circumstances where income redistribution is warranted, many cases exist in which it is totally inappropriate.

So, we begin by drawing a distinction that will surprise some readers. It is based on the answer to the following question: Are we *always* responsible to contribute to the well-being of strangers? The answer depends on the circumstances.

Let us recall that people are motivated to act as a result of two influences: their natural inclinations (which vary across individuals) and their moral feelings, which we argued should depend upon the reasoning powers of persons—since that is what makes us unique as human beings. (Fear and hope, guilt and peer-pressure are aspects of natural inclinations—in addition to obtaining pleasure and avoiding pain—when engaging in an action. Yet these psychological elements can be overruled by careful thinking and reasoning.)

We assume that our reasoning powers are similar enough across people (barring some cases of serious mental deficiency). Since most individuals have reasoning powers, we view the obligation to defend personal freedom to be based on two central ideas: that rules cannot be self-contradictory, and that no matter how well human decisions are made (in a world of uncertainty) no one knows for sure the outcomes of those decisions. Hence, the dignity and respect that we confer on others' choices must be based on their reasoning abilities and the significant uncertainties that they face when making their decisions.

Therefore, the most important right conferred on adult human beings has to be the right to self-actualization and self-ownership, for otherwise human choices are both restrained and lacking in accountability. Few people would doubt that the abolition of slavery in America and elsewhere in the world was an example of moral progress, for slavery was and remains the opposite of self-determination and self-ownership. In the American Southern states, in particular, slavery was especially onerous because slaves could neither try to improve their human capital via education and training, nor could they buy their own freedom. All that the slaves could do was escape to the North and hope that the legal system would protect their personal freedoms once they got there. In moral terms, it goes without saying that slavery was an abomination and that no property rights on slaves should have ever been extended to anyone.

But now we want to raise a broader (anthropological) question: Could there be an institution worse than slavery itself? It is not widely recognized that the right to slave ownership conferred some degree of protection to the slaves themselves. For there have been institutional arrangements that are worse than slavery, even though these are hardly known to the average American. Such an institution was the "encomienda" system that was practiced by the Spanish Empire in Latin America. In this case, the conquistadors would be granted transitional ownership over villages, and their control would last for a limited time period—as short as six months in the early colonial period! Then the villages would be turned over to another conquistador, regardless of the numbers of people left alive when the transition was made.

Imagine that! Human beings were under the control of a master for a limited period of time. This meant that the human assets could be exploited literally to the death, if necessary, to obtain the greatest economic return on them. The irony of it all is that the institution was defended by the Spanish Crown on the basis that it *prevented* slavery—but it was worse than slavery! The conquistadores themselves hated it and so did the aboriginal people, who had they been given the choice between encomienda and slavery, would have chosen slavery.

But slavery itself was an abomination. The question then looms: How could slavery be eliminated in a humane way that avoided conflict and death? The answer is obvious once we learn to recognize that private property rights *are a tool to bring about moral progress*. The slaves could be bought and given their freedom, as it was done in the English Caribbean; or the slaves themselves could be given the right to purchase their own freedom, as it was done in the late Spanish Empire, before general emancipation. This practice was not uncommon among the Romans. Why was this not seriously considered and applied in America?

The problem arose with the original contract that the Northern and Southern states agreed upon with the ratification of the original Constitution. While it was true that this document provided for alterations to its terms via the amendment process, doing so was extremely contentious because it affected the economic interests of Southern planters. The people in the North could not see themselves buying off chattel just to give the slaves their freedom. The tragedy was that in the absence of slave purchases, a Civil War followed, costing many times the amount that buying and freeing the slaves would have cost. The actual cost of the Civil War was not just monetary but in lives lost, a century of enmity between the North and the South, the establishment of transitory political decrees (such as the right to vote) that would soon be extinguished by Reconstruction (with the deplorable "Compromise of 1877"), and the permanent physical and mental disabilities (resulting from wounds and post-traumatic stress disorders) that affected both the civil and military populations for decades after the war.

Although this is an extremely emotional topic for all Americans, it needs to be faced front and center. Given that slaves could be bought, *they should have been bought back and given their freedom*—for then the Civil War would have been avoided. Once a contract (the Constitution) was signed and implicitly allowed for slavery, the right to purchase property could have been used to eliminate this abomination. It was done by others, including the English; historically, this was also practiced by the Romans, who allowed it at an individual, discretionary level.

When the right to property is respected *as an aid in the fulfillment of freedom* and not just the development of personal talents, conflicts can be avoided *at a price*, of course. Slaves should have been given their self-ownership, on moral grounds. This did not require the love of others (although that could have helped in accepting the economic sacrifice that had to be made) but rather the recognition of an obligation to free men and women because we, free men and women, demand freedom for ourselves. The avoidance of contradiction in our morals guides us to proper action. Duty calls, but this call is sometimes too much to bear: that is why the North was unwilling to pay for the slaves (while the South was unwilling to give them up for nothing). If property rights had been respected, and people had understood that their moral obligation overrode their personal happiness and well-being, the Civil War would have been avoided.

Sometimes, like in the case of slavery in America, morality requires the acceptance of a signed contract (the Constitution), followed by the economic sacrifice of purchasing the slaves, and the provision of their freedom. This is a clear cut case where we individuals are responsible for the well-being of others because within the lands under federal sovereignty "We the People" demanded self-ownership for all. Even when the rulers did nothing, it could or should have been in the hearts of moral people to form voluntary organizations to purchase the freedom of slaves. Moral rules bind individuals, independently of how the political collective wants to act. Surprisingly, people justify their individual immoral behavior on the basis that the collective fails to do what is right.

Let us consider a different situation. It is quite real indeed (as it will become clear) but it is presented as a fictional story. It has to do with the rescuing of stranded skiers after an avalanche—a policy which we oppose, on moral grounds.

Suppose that you, the reader, were skiing in a mountain and heard the thunder of an avalanche—but by luck you stood on a crag not impacted, even though close enough to the disaster. If after the avalanche has settled you continue skiing and on your path you encounter someone who has been seriously hurt by the avalanche, most likely you will do everything in your power to rescue that person. The healthy skier has no other choice, for this is a hurt human being deserving the same dignity that you, the healthy skier, want conferred upon yourself in similar circumstances. The sense of duty, which originates in morality, requires no less because suddenly the healthy skier has the opportunity to become a Good Samaritan.

Why, then, should we oppose the rescue of stranded skiers, yet be more than willing to rescue one if we encounter such a person after a natural disaster? Don't we have a duty to help any person in distress? The answer to this question is equivocal. On the one hand, we have a Biblical injunction to "love your neighbor as yourself." And following the Golden Rule, if we encounter a person in distress, we have the obligation to help that person, because we expect (and want) that the same person acting from moral reasons will do the same for us, if they found us in similar circumstances.

And yet, on the other hand, if *we do not encounter* such a person in distress, and that person is "there"—namely, in a dangerous situation where the risk of a disaster is well known and subject to calculation—then we can argue that the person in distress had the duty to protect himself or herself through insurance, and we have no obligation to search, rescue, or give any financial assistance for the recovery of that person. This reaction can also be derived from the Golden Rule! If I voluntarily engage in a risky activity, I have the responsibility to love my neighbors (and fellow citizens) by not imposing upon them the costs of the risks that I take. An ethics of responsibility involves being accountable (and liable) for the acts which I freely choose to take.

It should be obvious to all that one can predict the occurrence of avalanches, for specific slopes and regions. That being the case, the skiers themselves should absorb the costs of their rescues when avalanches come, and they should pay in advance for that cost. People want to drive and they know that the probability is greater than zero that they will suffer an accident; hence the collective forces the person to purchase insurance or to self-insure. Those who drive fewer miles pay lower premiums, and those who drive many miles pay higher premiums. The relative risks among drivers can be determined with great precision, and those risks can and should be included in the premiums that people pay.

The same should hold true for all risky activities as long as the risks are predictable. People should purchase the insurance or they should self-insure. When this is not done, the state that pays for the rescues imposes upon citizens a great harm, for they are forced to pay via taxation (which is coercive) for the natural inclinations of others—and that has nothing to do with any universal moral law.

In real life, governments tend to subsidize those who are reckless in their behaviors—either those who climb mountains, engage in skiing, live in floodplains and/or hurricane-prone or earthquake-prone areas. The rest of us have to pay for rescues and asset reconstruction. When we grant all people the dignity that is due their humanity, which is the right to choose freely, as their reasoning power allows and their natural inclinations directs them to, they must face the consequences of their decisions—*which we should all respect but not subsidize, unless doing so voluntarily* (as an act of kindness, but not as an obligation with an attendant duty).

Rulers, who have the power to coerce taxation, do not view this issue from a moral perspective. Such incidents allow them to appear to be benevolent rulers that provide for rescues and asset recoveries at no cost to the victims of predictable accidents. Economists argue against such behavior on the grounds that it creates what is called *moral hazard*, which is another way of saying that such subsidies encourage risky behavior. Since the cost is lower than the benefit to the risk takers, rulers allow or even contribute to the misallocation of resources. In contrast to economic theory, however, we argue that the real problem is far more than moral hazard, but includes an institutional structure that creates a form of dependency and disempowerment (veering to slavery) among the rest of us, since we are forced to yield to strangers, against our will, resources that we have accumulated for the achievement of our own self-actualization.

This approach to our moral obligations makes it clear that in no way are we coercing people not to take risks. As we have emphasized, almost all behaviors involve an element of uncertainty. However, when that uncertainty can be calculated and becomes a determinate risk, then the person engaged in the activity has a responsibility to purchase insurance or to self-insure. A person who loves skiing has the legal and moral right to engage in that activity, as long as he or she purchases insurance and leaves other people's personal welfare out of the picture. He or she even has the right to be in love with that activity and teach it to his or her children, friends and neighbors. The person may be the most caring and selfless individual in the whole world—but that does not justify infringing upon other people's rights.

Slavery, if such an institution were to exist in any community today, is within a totally different moral context. The slave is a slave because of the power of the ruler (or oligarchy) to allow such an institution to exist. The condition of the slave—enforced disempowerment—is different because his or her condition is a violation of his or her dignity as much as mine, for we all demand the right to use our reasoning power to make the choices that have uncertain outcomes and make us free. We have *an obligation* to set him or her free, even if it involves our own financial sacrifice. This is sufficient proof that the moral life is independent of personal economic well-being.

The moral rule, then, regarding helping others is simply this. When we find an individual who is unable to help himself or herself (due, for example, to slavery, physical or mental incapacities, or age), we must treat that person as an end and not as a means. He or she is deserving of our assistance, both personal and collective. However, when the individual is an adult of normal mental capacity and engages in risky behaviors that he or she has chosen freely, then the individual does not deserve free assistance from anyone; he or she has the moral obligation to purchase an insurance policy that prevents the rest of us from facing the liabilities that he or she incurs.

We can hold indeed the position that everyone should try to reach self-actualization and still maintain a moral duty towards others; but this holds for everyone, and a reciprocal behavior must be expected. The conflict among people arises when some take up activities which are risky and yet are unwilling to be covered by insurance. It is true that we have the responsibility to help others due to no fault of our own or even theirs, but that is why we also state that there is an uncertainty in the world associated with everyone's actions, and *that uncertainty* we cannot eliminate. Once we understand the difference between risk and uncertainty, we can declare ourselves free from helping others who are unwilling to pay for the risks that they take—and the same applies to us.

Chapter Six

Private Property
Expands Our Opportunities

Having made the case for limited government and a universal ethics that demands personal responsibility, we now take the first step towards developing an institutional structure that allows for personal self-actualization while maintaining liberty, equality of access and civil independence. We will argue that private property rights are the foundations for such institutional structure. Yet, a fundamental question needs to be addressed: How is it possible to justify private property rights within the universal ethics that we have proposed? Regrettably, this simple question requires a complex answer.

We note that people often find themselves in conflict with their own natural inclinations, such as now, because while they find private property rights useful in practice, these rights appear to clash with some innate moral principles. Why is that so?

Let us begin the analysis with the right to own land. We soon discern that our property rights to this asset are secured by the state. Yet most states arose, historically, not through the consent of those governed by the state but rather by the use of force. Land was first owned by rulers, and it took a long time before the right to this asset extended beyond the ruling class. Historically, then, land ownership arose as a privilege rather than as an individual right that resulted from ethical considerations.

We also acknowledge that long-standing states required the use of force to bring together many disparate people, who did not give their consent to be governed by their rulers. The inclination to dominate others is easily explained (but not justified) by the natural propensities of people (and even animals living in packs). In fact, all animals that live in groups experience hierarchical controls. Rulers came to be rulers by force and coercion: They happened to be the strongest or smartest within their groups, and land owner-ship became the means to acquire and control wealth.

It is also true that people have other natural propensities, including the need to justify their religious feelings and their moral values. The problem is that most people rarely know how to justify their religious convictions or their moral values! Furthermore, in the age of science and technology, nei-ther faith nor tradition are enough to defend one's convictions on rational grounds. The best that people can do is to argue that these religious and moral convictions arose as a result of evolution. Let us explain.

Some argue that natural selection has made it possible to develop these natural personal feelings and propensities. While this type of arguments is appealing, it involves a contradiction because nature makes humans and animals to try to dominate others; nature does not restrain humans from engaging in ferocious warfare, or animals from destroying one another. Yet it is claimed, somehow, that nature creates in us religious and moral feelings and propensities that contradict other feelings and propensities that are equally natural in us. Theories with internal contradictions are not credible.

Clearly, reasoning powers can be used to promote both good and evil, terms which are defined by reason itself. Hence it is possible to argue, as was done in a previous chapter, that reason is something which has its own intrinsic worth that requires cultivation for its own sake. While reason can be used instrumentally, to figure out which are the correct means to achieve particular ends, the cultivation of reason serves to separate humanity from the animals because it gives us the ability to distinguish between right and wrong.

While it is true that all humans engage in self-love and self-centered projects, we argue that reason can convince us that we have the moral duty to respect the self-love and self-centered projects of others, for otherwise we cannot be consistent in justifying our own self-love and self-centered pro-jects. Our reasoning powers tell us that we should not engage in contradic-tion, and if we believe in our personal rights to protect and develop our own potential (which is what self-love and self-actualization is all about) we cannot deny that same right to others. In other words, our sense of being human depends on our reasoning powers, and these cannot justify contradic-tory statements, rules or proposals.

There are many advantages to making reason the justification for our moral values. First, it explains the personal conflict between our natural physical inclinations and our moral intuitions and feelings; reason keeps reminding us that if something is good for us, it can be good for others, too. Second, this perspective reflects a principle that is common among religious believers, who argue for human equality before God, a transcendental being. Reasoning (through its demand to avoid contradiction) requires the equal treatment of all human beings, not just before a transcendental being, but among us and before the law. Third, this perspective allows for a unique understanding and interpretation of the past and the current situation in which we find ourselves—especially with regard to individuals' private property rights, which is the subject of this analysis.

We do not need to justify on moral grounds the origin of most states and the usually oppressive rights to private property that their rulers developed. Rather, we need to accept as fact the historical success of someone or some group of people in creating states for personal gain and for misusing the right to property—for this right was made exclusive rather than universal, thereby contradicting reason itself. We realize that the original states were far from moral entities, and that our moral values (based on universal principles) would be at odds with the legal strictures of those states and would demand something akin to rebellion against those states—even when their establishment led to some positive consequences. Rebellion, the way we use this term, does not mean revolution and violence: it means that we had, and we continue to have, a moral duty to make *our* state conform to *our* moral values.

How can that be done? Or, alternatively, how has that been done? There is no doubt that some states have evolved closer to the universal demands of our moral precepts. For some philosophers, the first thing to do might be to determine the type of state that is desired. This might be done by thinking of an original contract (possibly under a veil of ignorance) that the citizens of the state would have agreed upon by unanimous consent. One could then proceed with speed and absolute determination to the replacement of the flawed existing state with a "better" political state—that is what revolution is all about.

The problem with this approach is two-fold. Revolutions beget violence and the violation of the moral rights of people, for in most cases people are not treated as entities with an intrinsic human dignity (based on their reasoning powers) but rather as representatives of particular groups, classes or ideologies that demand "special rights." Worse yet, whatever ideal state or rules that we can think of, our imaginations are always constrained by our ignorance of that which is possible. Therefore, ultimately, even ideal states and rules of governance in their utopian purity will have to be changed. The last thing we should desire is a situation with perpetual revolution and carnage, always done in the name of justice.

Such situation, sadly, was the one in which the 1789 French Revolution evolved. After trying to resolve the financial crisis by political means, such as the abolition of serfdom and unfair taxes, it ended up abolishing the proper forms of representation of individuals. This immediately led to Robespierre's "tyranny of virtue," which was coeval with the "Terror," and the horrendous carnage at the guillotine in which not only were innocents sacrificed to the suspicions of a few, but even the revolutionary devotees became the targets of the next wave of "true" revolutionaries. Modern revolutions (except for the American one) have repeated such a pattern of destruction of innocent bystanders and willing actors.

We argue—very much in line with Kant and the American Founding Fathers—that the means to achieving a moral state is far more important than our current vision of what that state will look like, no matter how clever we think we are. It is impossible to predict the technologies and overall circumstances (namely the constraints) that people will confront in the future. Since reason makes us aware of this uncertainty, it is wise to incorporate that uncertainty into our moral values and even our institutions.

People use their reasoning powers to make choices. Reasoning and choice are necessary to one another. When there is a natural law that cannot be avoided (and there is no uncertainty about this law, such as gravity) there is no purpose in engaging in self-reflection about it. We can, however, use reasoning when we perceive the possibility of overcoming the effects of a physical law. Reasoning is a tool for both making choices and for creating choices, when uncertainty is present. Reasoning about options and possibilities contributes to making people free in an uncertain world, and it also contributes to increasing the intrinsic worth of mankind.

No matter how carefully we think about our choices and possibilities, the fact remains that we are uncertain about any and all outcomes. It is on this basis that we must respect the integrity of individual choices, for each one of us is free to make the choices that in light of our reasoning powers are appropriate for us. Therefore, if we have the opportunity to create the rules or laws of the state, we must always protect the basic integrity of human reasoning and choices. The state must restrain individuals only when they infringe on the rights of others. Regrettably, most states (for a reason deemed raison d'état, the strange precedent that the state always knows better, no matter what) trample on the rights of people.

How, then, can me make an amoral state conform to our moral values? History provides us with a clue: Implement, defend and extend the right to private property. Make the right to private property a universal right. For understandable reasons, our Declaration of Independence only says "that [men] are endowed by their Creator with certain unalienable Rights, that among these are Life, Liberty and the pursuit of Happiness." While the founders could not imagine that one day people would not know how to justify the existence of a Creator, their argument should have read that we "have the Right to Life, Liberty and Private Property (including self-property) so that we can pursue the attainment of our human potential."

The Declaration excludes private property because of the then existing institution of slavery, which was an abomination. We argue that this modified statement can guide us in the progression towards a moral state. Regrettably, on the heels of this first flaw, our Founding Fathers were also unable to anticipate that future governments could use the promotion of happiness as a means of preventing people from attaining their human potential.

The individual, by himself or herself, can barely attain self-actualization or productivity. The individual needs not only himself and other people (who can be hired by means of voluntary agreements), but should and need to control physical and abstract assets to attain self-actualization and productivity. Historically, the extension of the right to own and acquire private property—to peasants, minorities, women and all human beings—has expanded the choices that people make, and the possibilities that they create for themselves. Slavery is an abomination precisely because it negates the most basic of human rights: to own oneself. Communist regimes are an abomination because all is owned by the de facto ruler, whether this is a politburo or a council of state, denying people the right to make choices for themselves.

Getting closer to an ideal moral state (where people have the maximum freedom to exercise their reasoning powers and make choices without impinging on the rights of others) has happened in historical time—but the reverse is also true. When we get closer to the ideal moral state, we observe restrictions on the Sovereign who created the state by force and coercion; property rights expand widely and can be obtained via purchases in voluntary exchanges. When we get away from the ideal moral state, the Sovereign expands its powers and makes choices that it feels benefit its own interests, and justifies those choices by claiming that they are the choices that people should make—if they were as wise as the Sovereign itself. The sale of assets is either prohibited or circumscribed to a limited number of people, and voluntary exchanges are disallowed.

There is no doubt that in the process leading to an ideal moral state we would observe the inequality of asset holdings, for this would reflect both the limits that yet exist on the acquisition of property and the inequality of natural talents that are distributed in the population. It may well happen that, in the future, natural talents can be enhanced and equalized—yet, even then, as long as goods and services are unequally valued by the population and voluntarily exchanged, the inequality of asset holdings will prevail.

In conclusion, while we understand that the control of assets via property rights enhanced the choices of rulers (who could then build monuments to themselves in the old days, or presidential libraries in our own days), our reasoning powers demand as a matter of consistency that all human beings should have similar rights to the acquisition and accumulation of property, in order to advance their own potential. These rights must be acquired and exercised via a peaceful process, whenever possible. Violence can only be justified in self-defense.

Yet, even those individuals who accept the idea that private property rights enhance the opportunities of those acquiring them may, or may not, accept the idea that those rights should be passed on to heirs. Therefore, we must deal with the rights to inheritance. The reader will find our conclusions complex and surprising.

Chapter Seven

Imposing Restrictions on Inheritance

We warn the readers that this chapter is by far the most controversial one in the book. That is not surprising, since political arguments about estate and inheritance taxes lead to heated discussions reflecting deeply held partisan beliefs.[1] We would also inform the readers that these taxes are paid by relatively few people; that the tax rates are highly progressive (in large part because only the well-off tend to pay any of them); and that there is a huge amount of tax avoidance which occurs as a result of the many loopholes in the tax code.

From our perspective, estate and inheritance taxes can reduce income inequality, especially across generations. Hence they are used as rhetorical tools in the arsenal of political campaigns, and to talk about them in a rational manner becomes practically impossible. However, since our goal is not to score political points but rather to find justification either for or against these taxes, we are willing to take the heat that this chapter will generate. The consequences of our proposals are as follows: (a) inheritance and estate taxes would mainly disappear; (b) they would be replaced by taxes (large or small, depending on the outcomes of the political process) on gifts, which would close the loopholes and significantly expand the tax base, meaning the number of people taxed; (c) force people to make very specific plans before their elderly years; (d) create a conceptual framework that could easily be applied to the allocation of assets after divorce; (e) force couples to sign prenuptial agreements; and (f) eliminate most of the jobs done by tax lawyers and tax planners.

All of the above consequences are drastic indeed, but they demonstrate our commitment to find a middle ground between political partisans. The middle ground is based on philosophical judgments, and not only are the arguments unheard of in normal political discourse, but they may appear to be insensitive, if not repressive towards children and the elderly in particular, and even spouses (male or female) that do not participate in the labor markets. It is not our intention to offend anyone: we simply allow the arguments to lead our discourse. It is now time to begin.

It may be said, without much exaggeration, that the greatest threat to the public's acceptance of private property rights is the existing legal rights to inheritances. While most people feel comfortable accepting that those who work very hard, or make breakthroughs in the economy as entrepreneurs, deserve to keep a substantial part of the wealth that they helped create, many people either resent or plainly reject the idea that wealth should be passed on to the descendants of the rich, who neither contributed to nor are likely to make good use of that wealth. Sometimes even the rich accept this rejection, giving away most of their wealth to their favorite charities rather than to their own spouses or offspring (who might just get small inheritances).

If we go back to the creation of states, property allowed for the perpetuation of the status quo. Kings, nobles and masters inherited property, which literally allowed them to control the opportunities that were available to others. Taking that into account, we have argued before that those others could improve their own condition only if and when they obtained rights to private property themselves. The extension of private property rights to all citizens has been painful yet necessary to get to where we are today—and much more can be done. Yet, inheritance remains an actual or potential impediment to equality of opportunity for all. This chapter deals with inheritance, not with voluntary exchanges of money for property.

Even though he was a major defender of private property, Immanuel Kant made the point in his work *The Doctrine of Right* that the rights of inheritance were entirely determined by the state, and offered no guidance about those rights.[2] Private property allows the individual to use his talents both to improve himself and to improve the economy—by allowing for the better allocation of resources. (Note that people generally acquire property for a price that is higher than the value it has to the original owners, an indication that the property can be put to a better use. That is why the resale of property can improve the allocation of resources, as long as people are not deluded or misinformed.)

But even when and if these arguments are accepted, it is not clear that anyone's descendants, or for that matter, anyone who is given property as a gift, has a right to control any property that he or she has not caused to grow. The one reasonable exception is when a person dies and leaves behind underage children (less than 18 years old), when the creation of a limited-life trust can be justified, and the property itself is managed by experts.

Let us now make the distinction between the acquisition of property via inheritance, and the acquisition of property via gifts. Since children are not likely to be productive (with some minor exceptions) and they have the right to be taken care of by their parents (or even by the state) before the attainment of adulthood, the argument can be made (with the exceptions for child prodigies), that children have no right to own property at all. If children are underage and get an inheritance, "their" property can be managed by experts, until they turn 18. If children are adults and receive a gift from their departing parents, there is no reason at all not to tax that gift.

While this may be a fairly unpopular position to take, its unpopularity resides not in the principle involved, but rather in the tax laws that permit lower taxation of income when children, or their trusts own property. Middle and upper class families love to set up trusts for their children, because they take advantage of tax loopholes that lead to lower taxes. But we contend that this behavior violates a fundamental principle which is essential in the defense of private property rights; namely, that only those who can be potentially productive with their property have a right to it. This does not mean that the state should take away property from adults who consistently make mistakes; most likely, in those cases, they will lose some or all of their property anyway. We argue, instead, that private property has to be tied to those who make decisions about it, thereby (and potentially) making a productive use of it.

When property is tied to decision-makers and nothing else, a set of unexpected consequences follows. If a decision maker is divorced (or dies), for example, and the spouse (man or woman) has not contributed in any significant way to the property's acquisition or growth, then there is no obligation for the legal system to declare that the spouse has a right to the property. (Contributions may be direct or indirect. A spouse who works in the business, for instance, is making a direct contribution to the value of that business; and a spouse who invests in his or her mate's education deserves a return to his or her investment.) Of course, once this principle is accepted, marriage contracts should be drawn and renewed on a yearly basis, establishing how much a spouse is contributing to the other's assets, just in case a divorce or death happens. (Surprisingly, this could benefit the nuclear family, as it reassesses yearly its financial health.) If a mate is not contributing to the growth of an asset, the distribution of assets will be seen as gifts rather than inheritance, and then the state will have a right to tax this gift.

Underage children would not be treated like spouses, given the obligation that parents have to support their children. Spouses who contributed to the development and growth of the property must retain their contribution to that property and face no taxes. When we tie property to those who make decisions about it, this by itself prevents the placing of property in trusts while the parents are alive. This does not mean that a wealthy individual may not use the services of others to manage his or her property, but that he or she must be the ultimate decision maker of the use of his or her property. For let us face it, trusts are financial fictions that allow the wealthy to pass on property to their descendants either free of taxes or through the payment of minimal taxes. We advocate the use of trusts only for underage children whose wealthy parents have actually died.

Furthermore, it must be recognized that the true elderly, unless they are in exceptional health and have exceptional clarity of mind, are also unable to take responsibility for their own property (except their homes). If children are unable to own property, then the elderly should not be allowed to own property either, unless they can manage it and can prove that they can do so. This restriction will not deprive the elderly of income, as we shall explain below. Would this change their lifestyles? Not at all.

We argue that if the elderly have no income from their savings, the productive citizens of the state have an obligation to provide the elderly with the financial means to maintain a reasonable life style. The reason for this is that we would expect others to take care of us if similar circumstances arose. When, on the other hand, the elderly have savings and properties that extend beyond their home, they still deserve financial assistance from the state commensurable to the taxes that they paid during their lifetimes (since they contributed to the welfare of others while they worked as adults). The elderly should also have the right to purchase annuities that will provide them with additional income. But when a person cannot manage his or her property, then he or she should not have the right to own it, period.

All citizens, then, must have a plan for themselves when they become elderly. Starting at some pre-determined age (we would propose 78; or 60 years past 18, the age of adulthood), those who are property owners must prove that they can personally manage all of their properties (even with the assistance of others, but never in trust), or otherwise their properties are sold and/or turned over as gifts to descendants, friends, charities or whatever, as designated by the previous elderly owners.[3] This would apply not only to physical assets, but also to stocks and bonds. If the properties are sold, the former owners may keep some or all of the money, yet retain the option of acquiring (some or many) annuities that will provide them with additional income during the remaining years of their lives. If the elderly decide to have large amounts of money holdings at their disposal past the age of 78, rather than annuities, the "inheritors" must pay gift taxes on those accounts when they receive the money as gifts.

If the person proves to be competent (which would be determined by questioning how the properties are managed) then the process is repeated every ten years. If a person older than 78 dies while managing his or her assets, then all of the properties pass on to the state, which must in turn sell it within one year and use the funds exclusively for tax relief. Therefore, the political problem of property inheritance is resolved, for no inheritance is possible—except in the case of underage children and personal residences, to which no one objects.

This proposal may appear fanciful, but it does so only because people have never taken seriously that inheritance contradicts our basic justification for private property. Private property rights are there to allow individuals to improve themselves and make use of their talents. If they cannot do so (as in the case of most children and the truly elderly), then the property must be sold or passed on to others (except for their homes).

No one objects to the giving or receiving of gifts—and there is no reason why these should not be taxed, either. If a person wants to shower himself or herself with opulence (via huge annuities) while being elderly, that is also fine, but then the control of assets must pass on to a management firm that provides annuities and makes decisions about the use of the property. The only true inheritance that should be allowed is that of private homes (which need not be taxed as a gift when they are passed on as an inheritance).

The readers may be puzzled that authors who praise private property as essential to the attainment of human freedom and self-actualization, are so willing to impose restrictions on its use once an adult reaches a certain age— which has been suggested to be 78 (when most adults can still make careful choices). We recognize the arbitrariness of the age, but that arbitrariness can be moved up or down via the political process. Our argument is based on the idea that age makes a difference, and that everyone needs to be aware that abilities and intelligence diminish with age. There will be a few people who can still be highly productive past the age of 88, for example, but we must all recognize the physical and mental limitations that most people past 88 currently face. (The age of political correctness is rapidly disappearing.)

Hence we urge people to do something which on the surface seems to run counter to their own values: give up the administration of property at a certain age. It does not mean that they cannot hold on to their wealth—they can do so if they so desire, but only in the form of annuities and money holdings. Private property requires an active management, and those who have learned to administer property effectively must face the fact that such administration must be passed on to others—who happen, generally, to be younger. There is nothing said about the tax rate that must be used as a gift tax—which could be set at a relatively low or high rate. But if we want market institutions to work effectively and efficiently, assets must be managed properly, and that is our foremost goal.

Finally, those who pass on before the age of 78 could have their property distributed as gifts according to the plans that they had previously developed. The writing of these plans should be made mandatory for anyone holding wealth beyond a certain threshold. While these and prior proposals are unusual, we are confident that they are compatible with those of two great philosophers, Aristotle and Heidegger, but we will explain why in endnote 3.

Let us summarize our proposal. Inheritances (except for children below 18, and of private homes) give way to donations, all of which are subject to gift taxes. A person reaching the age of 78 (or thereabouts) must either donate all or part of his properties, or sell all or part of his properties and turn them into annuities and/or money holdings. If the person can prove that he or she is still capable of managing his or her properties, then he or she can continue doing so, but upon his or her death the properties are turned over to the government (except his or her home, which can be passed on to heirs) and sold in the marketplace, with the proceeds going exclusively for tax relief to the general population. The money holdings of the elderly are to be distributed as gifts, and those gifts are subjected to taxation.

Anyone living past 78 will have the right to receive a government pension commensurate with his or her previous tax history, and will have the right to keep and pass on his home to heirs. (Note that if the person is unwilling to make donations to others, or pass on anything to heirs at the age of 78, he or she can turn the properties into annuities and lead a luxurious life style until the person dies). The principle behind this proposal is simple: Private property rights are there to allow individuals to improve themselves and make full use of their talents. Nothing else justifies private property rights over assets. The taxation of gifts would be determined by the political process, which would reflect the political idiosyncrasies of the various generations. Tax lawyers and tax planners will find something better to do, from a social standpoint. And the rhetoric against income inequality will be substantially diminished.

Those who object to this proposal on the grounds that we extend the role of government in inheritance decisions forget that the government is already impacting our behavior with the tax code, plus poisoning the political discourse by allowing the well to do to engage in extensive tax planning and avoidance. We eliminate loopholes. We also want people to gain greater control over their lives by making decisions when they can still do so mentally and physically. The elderly often become dependent on people, even relatives, who do not have their best interest at heart. This painful truth shall make them free.

NOTES

1. For a general background on estate taxes, the reader can consult Chye-Ching Huang and Brandon Debot, "Ten Facts You Should Know About the Federal Estate Tax," updated March 23, 2015, accessed October 27, 2015, http://www.cbpp.org/research/ten-facts-you-should-know-about-the-federal-estate-tax.

2. Kant's endorsement of the fundamental reforms of the French Revolution focused in part on the abolition of so-called Special Orders and their privileges, including their property holdings and titles passed on through inheritance. The special rights of primogeniture were also at the forefront of what the British Whigs objected to in the monarchy. Thus, on account both of Kant and Locke, we believe that revisiting the issue of inheritance is warranted. "We the People" desire both reform and a more perfect union, which necessitates changes in the laws related to inheritance.

3. To Aristotle, excellence in the city cannot be accessible to children or even young adults, but only to mature individuals; on the other hand, the elderly could not be counted to make valid decisions about going to war. Heidegger argued that the authentic life of a person is revealed when the individual accepts and confronts his or her mortality, which is not generally done by the average person. Our proposals, in a sense, force individuals close to the age of 78 to accept and confront their mortality.

Chapter Eight

Using Property Rights to Better Understand Abortion and Adoption

The issue of abortion presents a dilemma when viewed from the moral perspective of this work. Can the fetus, as a potential human being, have someone claiming on its behalf a right to stewardship, while at the same time the mother of that fetus have indisputable rights to her self-ownership? These stewardship and ownership rights can be in conflict with one another if the mother considers having an abortion, which terminates the life of the fetus. We must explore, then, how the conflict of rights can be resolved.

The dilemma has an element of surprise in the sense that in all cases (except rape) the fetus does not come into being without an implied consent from the mother. Rapes regrettably come in different varieties—they may be done by a stranger, a friend or even a family member who is abusing a (child-bearing) woman. These cases are by far the most difficult to resolve, for neither the mother nor the fetus is responsible for the consequences of the rape. Both the mother and the fetus are victims of an evil act and, while the mother has every right to distance herself from the consequence of the act—by having an abortion—the fetus should also receive some consideration as a victim of the act. The tragedy is so immense to both entities that one feels totally helpless in trying to determine the correct moral position.

Yet, most abortions are not the response to rape. The closest analogy that one might make of those abortions is the following. Imagine if one temporarily disabled person is forced into another's home, yet later the homeowner demands the visitor to leave, at a time when the disabled visitor is unable to do so. The homeowner then claims that the visitor can be killed because he or she has failed to leave the home when demanded to do so. While one can

61

understand the demand of the homeowner to have control over her privacy, one must recognize that the disabled visitor is there involuntarily and deserves not just compassion, but respect. The moral dilemma occurs when the sexual act is consensual, and yet the fetus (what we have called a temporarily disabled person) is rejected after that consensual act. In that case, those of us who put a high value on human potential and personal responsibility must try to find a non-coercive solution to the problem.

The above approach is often rejected when the fetus is only considered a "thing" or a "blob" analogous to a tumor, cancerous or not. However, this "thing" or "blob" ultimately turns into a human being who while within the womb is disabled—because an early birth will likely result in some disabilities. Yet even in this case, one has to raise the question of when the "thing" becomes a human being. We believe that the answer to that question depends on the medical technologies that are available to save the fetus outside the womb; once the knowledge of that timing occurs, our analogy between the fetus and a temporarily disabled visitor gains support. We also note that— whether or not a woman wants an abortion—if her fetus is lost as a result of natural causes, the woman has not had an abortion but a miscarriage. There is no moral dilemma in this particular case.

Let us then assume that a fetus has reached viability outside the womb, which is now considered to occur within 21 to 24 weeks after conception, since some children have actually survived birth 21 weeks after conception. We must first make the case that no abortions should be sanctioned after that date; however, doing so requires us to convince mothers not to have an abortion (a) by devising an equivalency between pregnancy past 21-24 weeks and stewardship and (b) by facilitating the financial environment that will achieve that end. Other non-coercive means, of course, may be considered too.

The first part of our approach is to try to convince the mother—in connection with partner citizen groups—that she is actually performing a service (stewardship and surrogacy) for another couple that is interested in the adoption of the child. She could be encouraged to think of herself as a surrogate mother to another couple, who has provided her with an ovum and a sperm so that she can carry the pregnancy to term. This approach provides the mother with a different and positive perspective about her pregnancy; she becomes motivated with doing the right thing for persons other than herself, including her unborn child. No one needs to know the true circumstances of the pregnancy, and even those in the know will accept the change of status of the unborn, from personal ownership by the mother to her stewardship and surrogacy, for the sake of the life of the unborn.

Stewardship/surrogacy rights could be granted (after 21 weeks of pregnancy) to both the mother and the adopting couple, or an institution acting in behalf of adopting couples. The mother can be compensated for her humanitarian act, and the adopting couple could pay for the care and medical needs of the mother, who is carrying the pregnancy to term. While someone might argue that the process involves failing to reveal the truth, one could respond that the woman who engaged in the sexual act is, in fact, not the mother who allowed for the pregnancy to come to term. The first woman was unwilling to accept responsibility for her act, while the second one is a loving one who makes the best out of a difficult situation. We have a long tradition, in most cultures, to seek redemption for improper behavior. The mother, in particular, needs to be praised for her courage rather than be humiliated for an unwanted pregnancy. (This last statement should not be interpreted in any way as lifting moral responsibility for the sexual act by the mother's partner; both persons share responsibility for the birth of the child.)

The dilemma becomes far more complex when married couples, and not just single mothers, consider aborting an unborn child. When that occurs, it appears that the only non- coercive alternative is to give the state the right to issue a protective "insurance" on behalf of the unborn child, after 21 weeks of pregnancy. This insurance would be extended to the parents of all children after the 21-week period, and could be cashed in once the child is born. When that happens, the natural parents still have the choice of keeping the child or putting it up for adoption.

Now, there is no doubt that some couples will resist having the baby and refuse the state generated insurance payoff—and not much can be done in those cases, unless the state bans abortions after 21 weeks and establishes penalties for its occurrence. It may also happen that some couples decide to bear children just for the sake of the insurance payoff—but that can be resolved after cashing the insurance thrice, for the state could stop payments after three children. The importance of the approach is to convince the population that children are a most valuable blessing to society at large, and that mothers retain the right to have an abortion but only in the early stage (21 or at most 24 weeks) of their pregnancies.

Someone might object that reduction in the number of abortions would take place by money changing hands. But then, the question arises: Why, by and large, have we failed in the past to make use of money incentives as a resolution to one of our most difficult moral dilemmas? Both abortions and slavery could be reduced if people were willing to pay the price. (The issue with regard to slavery is discussed below.) Funding "orphanages" was (and in some countries remains) the price that some societies were willing to pay in order to prevent child murder. Money that is used to save the life of an innocent human being is not morally tainted in any way.

Regrettably, religious arguments to save the life of the unborn seem to have a limited impact everywhere—especially among the elite, whose politicians have transitioned (or have evolved, to use the preferred terminology these days) from being pro-life to being pro-choice. The media is almost entirely in favor of abortion, and the topic is not even discussed as a serious issue in the academic world. While the pro-life movement has won converts, particularly among the young, it has done so by means of emotional arguments which do not stand up to the scrutiny of academic discourse. Regrettably, too, when one proposes subsidizing mothers and couples for the birth of their children, the proponents are dismissed out of hand, as if buying lives was a banal activity.

Readers of this book should be convinced by now that, as a nation, our most difficult moral dilemma was slavery—which could have been resolved in a peaceful manner by the acquisition of slaves, the immediate remitting of their awful status, and their subsequent education and training. Yet, that was not done. Why? Because a majority of people consider their financial well-being more important than their moral obligations. The end result, of course, was a war that tore the country apart and led to thousands of injuries and deaths. No doubt, too, that this solution would have added to the amazing economic development taking place in the United States in the last one third of the 19th century.

If the life of the unborn is deserving of our protection we must, individually and as a group, protect it without precipitating unintended damage, caused by coercing women against abortions when they have a stake in their own personhood. Proper behavior can be *encouraged* in those who do not share our moral values, and all we need is our willingness to engage in financial sacrifice.

The irony of it all is that governments try to convert moral issues into political issues. This means that previous contracts are disregarded (like the acceptance of slavery in the original U.S. Constitution); that the rights of women are ignored in the case of abortion; and that the stake of the unborn is similarly ignored, as if stewardship was never needed. Moral issues demand our personal sacrifice and alertness, but not forced coercion by the state—for it is freedom that gives us our special significance as human beings.

Even if our approach encourages the birth of additional children, this is not a burden on most developed societies. Fertility rates across all of them are barely close to the replacement ratio—a sad situation characteristic of most European countries, Russia and Japan. In China, as a result of the "One Child Policy" the replacement ratio is not even achievable, and China may well become an old society before its people fully enjoy the wealth they've created. The one country that understands the importance of higher fertility rates for economic growth is France, which has established financial rewards for the birth of children.

It is sound policy to allow a country's population to renew itself with children born there, rather than with children or adults born outside its borders who share different cultural values that make governance even more difficult than it normally is. Our proposal is problematical only to those who believe that population growth is a curse—when, in fact, it is a blessing to countries that respect property rights and the dignity of human beings.

Our wealth comes from human ingenuity, the free and extensive exchange of goods and services (which itself depends on the size of the market), economies of scale and agglomeration, the right to property and its fruits, impartial supervision of the rules of the game and the defense of our borders. The more abundant a population we have in a country, if we keep our individual freedoms, the greater our prosperity and growth. Which choice should a hesitant woman make— one with an opportunity for a better financial life (as a result of monetary compensation for avoiding an abortion) while she also fulfills the dream of a barren or willing adopting couple? Or shall it be one with fewer opportunities and the never-disappearing psychological hurdle of knowing that she did not correct a mistake, but simply terminated it?

In conclusion, then, while we oppose restrictions on abortion past the 21st or 24th week of pregnancy (based on the rights of the mother to self-ownership), we find the practice abhorrent, and we urge private groups and even the government to search for financial alternatives that will end or diminish those abortions. We also believe that the moral issues involved should be addressed and discussed publicly in the academy, and we hope that this chapter serves as a step in promoting such discussions.

Chapter Nine

The Market Is the Best Engine for Conflict Resolution

We have argued so far that private property rights empower people, but these rights are normally held within the institutional structure that we call free markets. Regrettably, these markets are often corrupted by governments through special privileges granted to some in the form of payoffs and entitlements. People then face the dilemma of accepting competitive institutional structures or government handouts. These handouts are not "free" because someone else has to produce the goods and services, but the transfers occur when the government taxes Peter (the producer) to pay Paul (the consumer). This chapter, then, analyzes the web of taxation, hand-outs and markets that citizens find in everyday life. Our goal is to demonstrate that free market institutions need our protection, even when there are valid circumstances where income transfers are desirable. We begin our analysis with the issue of taxation.

Taxation diminishes our ability to achieve self-actualization, for the simple reason that it takes resources away from us. However, this does not mean that taxation needs to be abolished or necessarily (everywhere and in all cases) reduced. As we have pointed out in previous chapters, most people agree that we have a moral obligation to care for those unable to care for themselves, and possibly reducing disagreements, such as abortion, that involve conflicting rights. We are trying to determine taxation's proper scope and level—so that specific adjustments (downward or upward) can be considered. We first turn to history to showcase the iniquity of taxation.

Although this argument is seldom or ever made, slavery is a form of extreme taxation over the person made a slave, although the benefits accrue to individual slave owners, who typically (but not always, as we shall see) are part of the private sector. The slave masters collect many or most of the goods produced by the slaves, and use part of the revenue to maintain the workforce. Now—lo and behold!—communist regimes work under a similar institutional framework. All or most assets are owned by the state, which are then provided or assigned to the producing populations as their designated workplaces or housing units. The people are given a miserable percentage of their output in money terms, which they can use to purchase a few essentials for their well-being, or rather their survival.

People are amazed to learn, for example, that with the coming of the Raul Castro regime in Cuba in 2005, average wages were raised from $13 per month to $15 per month—and this "per month" clause is not an error in the text![1] Yet Cuban workers, together with the capital owned by the state, on average produced over $8,000 of output per capita per year.[2] When one considers that pensioners were receiving even less per month than the working population, it should be clear to the reader that the levels of taxation in Cuba are huge, and that when income transfers occur, they are entirely controlled by the state. These take the form of subsidized housing prices, food prices, "free" transportation and education, etc. In each and every instance, the point is that it is the state (like the overseer of the slaves) who gets to decide who benefits, when and in what proportion, with no input of opinion from the population, despite the fact that it is the workers who produce the output in terms of labor and work performance.

In the early days of the Castro regime, Cuban soldiers fought African wars of convenience for the USSR, and the country was paid off through huge subsidies by the Soviet Union. The so-called subsidies (which were compensation for the soldiers' work) were allocated to the population by the government. In modern times, Cuba sends large brigades of medical doctors to foreign countries, such as Venezuela and Brazil, and those medical specialists end up receiving a half (or less) of the payments that the Cuban government receives for their services. The rest of the income is distributed within Cuba as the governing elite sees fit. Why does such a system work? Three reasons come to mind. First, the population has no understanding of how the system works, which shows in the fact that when people in Cuba are asked about taxes they claim there are no, or few, taxes in the island! Second, there is no freedom of the press and no opposition to what the government disseminates through the press or through the schools (all of which are 100% government-controlled). And third, the people fully depend for their livelihood on what the government decides to give them: hence a culture of complete dependency has been established and is thoroughly institutionalized.

The consequences of this extreme example are that all decisions become political decisions, and that the power of the purse does not depend on productive activities but on political actions by the elite. This is the crucial point that we want to emphasize, to contrast this forced system of allocations (characterized by widespread "entitlements") with the allocation of resources in a market system. However, even the market system cannot exist without the government, because only the government can set rules and use coercion to enforce those rules. Hence all free market systems must exist within a mixed institutional structure.

When a person chooses to participate in competitive markets, this person knows that if he or she has the funds to purchase goods or services, they will be forthcoming. When the person lacks the funds, but has the potential to earn those funds and is willing to borrow the money, the goods or services will also be provided. The person will have to determine by himself or herself what is best, and must take the value of his or her time into account. The final choice is the individual's, and the individual's alone, for he or she chooses the optimal goods or services, finds the appropriate provider, and decides on the level of risk that the person will incur when the goods are used. That risk, too, can be insured in a market system. In return, the worker will have to provide labor services and be paid the market valuation of those services.

On the other hand, when an individual chooses the governmental provision of goods, whether he or she knows it or not, the "purchases" are in fact subject to a group decision—and the group or its representatives may or may not agree with him or her, providing or not providing the goods. The person may not even want to purchase the goods or services provided by government, for they may not be to the person's full satisfaction; yet he or she has to get the available items anyway. In fact, the person will likely not be able to determine the cost of the items, since the political process in a democratic society involves bargaining among representatives, and citizens end up paying not only for goods or services they want, but are being charged, via taxes, for other goods and services that they do not even contemplate buying.

The above remarks mean that purchasing through the market is not a contentious activity, whereas purchasing something via the political process inevitably leads to conflicts (whether fully acknowledged or perceived as rumblings). Representatives, even when best intentioned, do not know the exact tastes of people; providing, for instance, too much or too little educational services, health care, police protection, national defense, or whatever the good or service is provided by the government. Individual representatives are bound to reach agreements with others that end up providing too many government goods and services, for that is the only way to get approval for their own preferences in legislative bodies.

Why is it that the government provides so many goods and services? The answer is complex, for it involves a variety of factors. The government has the power to coerce taxes from people. This means specifically that if a majority of people want something, their representatives can force all the people to pay for it. This is nothing but the exercise of political power by special interest groups. It does not matter if a permanent minority is forced to pay for things it never wants: Taxes must be paid anyway. Political power extends over taxation proper, for the government can discriminate with regard to taxation too, and deliver goods to those who want them while forcing others to pay for them. (National parks, for instance, are rarely visited by the vast majority of people—and almost never visited by the poor, who cannot afford traveling to them).

Close to fifty percent of citizens do not pay any income taxes. This means that the other fifty percent must pay for many (or most) of the services delivered to "all," and in all cases they must pay for all services delivered to those not paying taxes. It should be noted, too, that payroll taxes are not quite regressive taxes, although they supposedly make the poor pay a higher proportion of income than is paid by the rich. The word "regressive" is a misnomer in this case because the benefits that accrue to people (as a result of these payroll taxes) are delivered, in much greater proportion, to the poor. For example, the poor are more likely to be ill in old age and the wealthy are more likely to be self-insured; hence the medical benefits paid out to the poor are generally greater than the medical benefits paid out to the wealthy.

In addition, many people work for the government. This means that not only do recipients of government goods and services get benefits, but the providers of government goods and services depend upon employment by the government itself. These people do not want to lose their jobs, and so are willing to vote for the provision of government goods and services, no matter how ineffective or inefficient that process becomes.

There is more. When the government controls education, and especially university education, government entities extend government largess by promoting research that is useless, but of interest to some party. At the lower educational levels, children are taught about the needs for, and benefits of, government goods and services, without ever explaining to them the costs (in alternatives foregone) of those goods and services. The universe of voters and the populace at large want to help the poor and downtrodden of the world, as long as they have no idea of the cost of such charity.

To be sure, the cost of government is difficult to quantify. Taxes imposed on some industry may be passed on to consumers, without the consumers realizing it. Also, taxes on some people can generate increases in measured income inequality, something that is totally disregarded in political discussions. For example, if some entity requires a $50,000 payment to provide specialized goods that could not be provided by someone else (say, abroad), and the government imposes a 50% income tax on the producer of the goods, then that entity will demand a $100,000 payment for the provision of the goods, to maintain a $50,000 net income for itself. In other words, taxation has the potential to generate greater and greater measured income inequality—which then justifies the imposition of even higher levels of taxes by future governments!

Since the government can discriminate among entities, determining winners and losers in the tax game, then these entities are forced to play the game—whether they like it or not. This means that resources are spent (usually via lawyers and experts in the appropriate field) on winning government contracts and favors. However, some winners are matched by some or many losers, and thus all the efforts by the losers go to waste. The wasted legal and expert services could have been used elsewhere, producing goods and services that the market would have allocated efficiently. In economics, this process of wasteful decision-making is called rent-seeking— whether it ends up in success or failure.

The government, too, should have no role to play in marriage controversies. Doing so imposes the equivalent of a tax burden on those with different opinions about marriage. Marriage is a contract for some traditions and a sacrament for others. In some countries and some traditions, these contracts and sacraments last for a limited time period, in others they last "until death doth [them] part." While we recognize that the state has a role to play in the education of children, and it is desirable to force parents to accept responsibility for the children they bring forth, the government has no role to play in deciding which religious or secular traditions are acceptable and which are not. The state should get out of the marriage business, saving the population millions in man-hours of controversial disputes.

While we want the government to disengage from purely ethical controversies, we see it engaged in education, where moral values are paramount. Most people want the schools to teach their children moral values, by teachers who have a deep knowledge and understanding of a variety of moral traditions. The subsidization of the public schools, which have an overwhelming secular framework, is a violation of the people's right to have their moral views and choices explained and presented to their children. In the current system, private religious education involves the doubling of educational costs, for parents pay both the taxes that go to the public schools and the costs of private education. The statistics provided for the costs of public education are totally misleading, too, for they never include the implicit and hidden costs of providing for the buildings, playgrounds, insurance, etc., that cities and towns pay for the maintenance of the educational infrastructure. These costs are not implicit or hidden in the case of religious schools and Charter Schools, making cost comparisons between public and private education meaningless.

The misallocation of resources by the government is hidden through the voting process. Let us explain. The political process is so convoluted that no one can be expected to be satisfied with its outcome. The vote for one or another politician is not a vote for this or that policy, for any single politician will have to take positions on hundreds of issues, affecting different groups in a variety of conflicting ways. Therefore, people become disenchanted, lowering their expectations for what politics can do for the state and the nation, and people withdraw into their private lives. People thus disenfranchise themselves, enabling plutocrats and demagogues to lord over them.

To put it more mildly, when people abandon the political arena, political interest groups fight it out with donations, campaigns, distortions and the imposition of rules that they can best control. For example, the creation of new political parties has become impossible in America. The only hope is to undermine one existing political party and take control over it. Once that happens, the incentives to gain power and control recreates the old institutional structures, where the newly elected politicians behave no differently than those they replaced.

One would actually expect local politics to receive the most attention of voters, but that is not the case, for voters have no practical way of becoming informed of the minutiae of local government. (They can comprehend even less the minutiae of state and federal governments!) Voters can be fully informed about their toothpaste or the apps of their iPhones, but are totally uninformed about what the local mayor or local council stands for. This exit or exile into private life is the worst outcome that must be avoided at all costs. Of course, politicians blame the voters for being uninformed when, in fact, their lack of information is the result of the institutional structure that the politicians, themselves, set up.

How, then, can this problem be resolved, or at least ameliorated? The answer is simply this: Allow the market to provide for as many goods and services as possible, and limit all governments to the most essential activities. Those are: national defense, the provision of justice, the establishment and enforcement of rules for market participants, the establishment and enforcement of minimal quality standards for goods and services, and the collection of taxes for running the government, among others. It may be necessary to provide some national, state and local goods and services that the private sector cannot provide, given the difficulty or high cost of collecting fees for them. Such may be the case for (most, not all) road construction and some types of truly public goods, such as weather forecasting, market information and predictions, border protection, police services, public health regarding issues of epidemic control and sanitation, etc.

We all share a moral intuition that government has a role in subsidizing poor children, the disabled and even the truly elderly, for they need and deserve our assistance; hence some level of bureaucracy is necessary to carry out these functions. But it should be clear to all that the greater the limits on governmental activities, the greater our satisfaction as consumers of private goods and services, which are the vast majority of the goods and services that we require. Our personal freedoms are inversely related to the size of government. Therefore, taxation must be limited to the same extent that useful government programs are limited.

Some—hearing the clamor from the demagogues or special interest groups—may claim that the market ignores the poor. This assertion is misleading. Throughout this work we have argued for the self-actualization of people, regardless of the income that they can attain. When a personal disability prevents someone from making it out of poverty, then government subsidies are in order. However, most poor people are poor not because of lack of abilities, but rather because of a lack of self-development, which normally requires the acquisition of skills and education. Poverty is more likely to occur as a result of growing up in a culture of poverty (and a culture of handouts) than a lack of personal abilities. Government programs keep people in poverty because they fail to provide the poor with incentives to acquire skills.

Being poor is not a disability, for if it were, the vast majority of our ancestors would have been disabled, and they were not. The difference between the old and the new generations is that the culture of handouts shows disrespect for the poor, humiliate them with dependency, and fails to express the sincere belief that they can come out of poverty through their own efforts. It is ironic that we have learned to treat the mentally and physically disabled much better than we treat the poor!

People would be scandalized if our political discourse emphasized the plight of the disabled the way we emphasize the plight of the poor. We have learned to recognize that different individuals have different talents, abilities and goals in life. If we hold this realization to apply to the disabled, why is it so difficult to do the same in the case of the poor?

The plight of the poor is aggravated mostly by our insensitivity towards them—by our consigning them to an entitlement mentality not merely from cradle to grave, but from generation to generation. The poor in this country, by all international standards, is far beyond the economic attainments of most of mankind.

It is true that the market is bound to lead to income inequalities—which can be ameliorated, not through a bureaucracy, but rather through establishing a culture that values attainment and excellence. The allocation of resources via the political process leads to rent-seeking activities by various special interest groups, the politicization of decision-making activities, the production and distribution of goods and services that citizens do not want, an educational system that violates the most elementary rules of educational services and freedom, and an economy that ends in stagnation.

Self-actualization leads to the acquisition of skills and knowledge, a reduction in poverty and an increase in freedom. In our view of an ideal society, the poor will only be those who have some personal disabilities (both physical and mental) that prevent them from participating—to the same degree as others—in the market process. Those individuals can and should be assisted by the state through income redistribution and a protective safety net—because that is the way we ourselves would like to be treated, if we found ourselves in those circumstances.

NOTES

1. The absurdity of low Cuban "salaries" continues being reported in the Western press. See Jessica Glenza, "Netflix launches $7.99 service for Cuba despite average wage of $17 a month" *The Guardian*, February 9, 2015, accessed October 31, 2015, http://www.theguardian.com/world/2015/feb/09/netflix-launches-streaming-service-cuba.

2. Per capita GDP in Cuba for 2010, in US dollars, was $10,200. See Central Intelligence Agency, *The World Factbook*, accessed October 31, 2015, https://www.cia.gov/library/publications/the-world-factbook/geos/cu.html. It should be obvious that workers (making up a bit more than fifty percent of the population) were on average producing close to $20,000 in yearly output; this means that the so-called "salaries" are figments of the imagination. As the text indicates, the problem in Cuba is that the levels of taxation are astronomical, and then the government transfers income to the workers via in-kind contributions of schooling, housing, healthcare, etc. Hence the word "salary" does not mean the same that it means in the United States. See Nicolás Sánchez, "Taxation Levels in Cuba and Other Topics of Rhetorical Interests," *Cuba in Transition*, 13 (August 2003): 103-114.

Chapter Ten

Discrimination as a Moral and Strategic Challenge

One could say that laws against discrimination are widely praised and accepted in our times. From our perspective, discrimination is against the moral values that we have developed so far. If one believes in the universal dignity of human beings and treats them as an end in themselves and not as a means, then discrimination is simply immoral.

Having said that, a very different question arises: Are laws against discrimination effective or even desirable? The answer may well be that they are not desirable, and that effective outcomes might be reached with a very different approach; namely, one that empowers buyers and sellers to make all the purchases and all the sales they want via voluntary transactions. Discrimination becomes a strategic challenge. Once again, let's take a look at the historical record.

The attempts to prevent discrimination, particularly against Jewish populations, have a long history in Europe. Given the constraints that were imposed on the economic activities of Jews, it was customary for Jewish leaders to purchase from the sovereign (by means of bribes and quid pro quo agreements) the expansion of their rights, allowing them to acquire property and to participate in most economic activities. The problem that the Jewish communities faced—or for that matter any group that attempted such a means of acquiring rights denied to them—was that when a sovereign granted the rights, the sovereign could also take them away. It has been impossible to purchase perpetual rights from any sovereign, for rulers are not only fickle, but in the end they all pass away.

It is always in the interest of sovereign authorities to grant and to take away rights from particular groups of people; when bribes are used to obtain rights, the threat of taking away those rights generates additional bribes. We must remember that discrimination can only be enforced via coercion, meaning that it can only be enforced by the power of the state. When discrimination exists only in the hearts of men, yet minorities keep the right to purchase those goods that some want to deny them and a few others keep the right to purchase the goods that minorities produce, discrimination vanishes; the process may take longer, but it is permanent—unless the state intervenes to prevent the right to purchase and sell the goods and services.

When Cuban refugees from Castro arrived in Miami, they found that they confronted housing discrimination. One of the authors of this book remembers how his family was unable to rent an apartment in a middle class neighborhood of the city. Yet housing discrimination soon evaporated. Why? The change could begin when an owner or manager feels empathy for the suffering of others. (In this writer's case, the owner of an apartment building was an Albanian whose family had gone through a similar exile experience many years before.) But it may also begin when an owner feels the need to make extra income by renting out empty properties, or renting out properties at a higher price. Whatever the reason, the market allows for the allocation of resources to those who value them the most. If nearby units are then vacated due to either racial discrimination or xenophobia, more and more units are opened up to minorities, as it happened to the Cuban refugees. There is no need to create anti-discrimination laws, or to bring to the fore the coercive apparatus of the state. The solution is to allow owners the right to rent out apartments as they see fit. Those who leave a neighborhood do so voluntarily.

Anti-discrimination laws can be defended when these invalidate covenants in deeds. These hidden clauses prevent owners from selling (or renting) to particular groups of people. When that happens, renters and buyers cannot exercise their demands for goods and services: discrimination is enforced by the coercive power of the state. There is no justification for forcing anyone to rent out or to sell to persons that owners do not like—regardless of the reason. Owners may be irrational from an economic point of view, but we as a community have the moral obligation to allow persons to determine how their property is being disposed of and used—making this a universal principle that applies to us and everyone else.

This precept is difficult for people to accept, and for its defense we return to history. The first sovereigns owned their lands because doing so gave them great power—in fact the power to control everyone, since people depended on land for their survival. However, once wars among sovereigns started, it became clear that they needed the cooperation of others, and hence they either formed coalitions (where the ownership rights of other sovereigns had to be respected) or gave away land grants to create a class of nobles who could help them in the defense of particular areas. Similarly, the needs and tastes of the nobles could only be met in some cases by the entrepreneurship of the middling class—the middle class of the entrepreneurs, doctors, inventors, artists, professors, etc.—who needed clear ownership of their assets, businesses and intellectual possessions. People acquire permanent rights only when people in power find it in their own interest to grant those rights.

When coercion is used, as was the case after the American Civil War, the granting of rights does not work. While we do not know exactly what would have happened to the black populations of the South if their liberty had been purchased, one can make the case that the evolutionary process would have followed the same course of events that was observed in the British Caribbean. We would have observed the slow integration of blacks and whites, greater migration of minorities to places with better economic opportunities, better racial relations and less bitterness between the populations of the North and the South. In addition, both the North and the South would have remained prosperous (in the absence of war) and would have provided better employment opportunities for all.

People believe that the racial "equality" achieved by blacks in modern America was the result of the Civil Rights Movement; we disagree. In our opinion, whatever improvements blacks have achieved have been the result of the need to recruit black soldiers to fight in the Second World War—and the need to keep blacks in the military to protect the country during the Cold War and the military interventions in Vietnam, Iraq, Afghanistan and Syria.

While there is no doubt that blacks achieved greater educational and training levels with the changes in educational opportunities, these arose because of the fear of a black revolution, which had become a near certainty with the military training of blacks, their violent demonstrations in the 1940s and 1950s, and their riots in the 1960s and 1970s. Numbers speak louder than words, when the minority populations are trained in the arts of war. But neither the fear of violence nor actual violence is ever conducive to better racial relations.

What is conducive to better racial relations is when private property owners figure out that it is profitable to hire blacks (and other minorities) because these can increase their investment returns. This development took place in both the entertainment and the sports world—and it would have been done earlier if the government had not been the enforcer of racial discrimination. Interestingly, sports owners allowed Latino players in their baseball teams, as long as they were white or passed for whites (even when they were not). In some cases, the players felt that they had to hide their Hispanic backgrounds, as was true with Ted Williams, who was a Mexican American player in the same sense that President Obama is an African American politician. Ted Williams' mother was a Mexican with deep ties to Mexico, where she and her parents were born. To this day, most Bostonians do not know this fact, and find the information objectionable or simply incredible.

Discrimination takes many forms, and sovereign authorities encourages them all. In contrast, when groups of people receive special consideration, they find some rationalization to justify it. There is no moral reason for the sovereign powers to grant special considerations on any group, yet this is done in the area of taxation—or the opposite, subsidization. Most Americans, for example, have to pay to mail letters, but that is not done by members of Congress, who are given franking privileges with minor restrictions, costing taxpayers millions of dollars. Newspapers, too, are subsidized via the postal service. Many people find this acceptable, on the dubious grounds that this secures or maintains freedom of the press—a freedom that is not extended, absurdly, to radio and television programs!

People interject their likes and dislikes for activities when judging the promulgation of legal rules, which must be universal in character if they are to pass a universal moral test. People do not fully grasp the danger of their behavior. Nonprofit institutions are either partially or totally exempt from taxation. This gives the governing authority the ability to regulate what these institutions can or cannot say, and makes the nonprofit sector complicit in supporting tax increases when the sovereign wants to do so. While it is true that some nonprofits battle the government on tax increases, no one misses the point that their credibility is damaged because they themselves have tax-exempt status!

Consider the following question: How many members of tax-exempt organizations argue that their institutions should lose their tax-exempt status? Once a person or group becomes a member of a privileged class, they defend their new status.

As a result of the arguments above, we assert that a moral state requires universal and proportional income taxation. We must respect the dignity of each human being, regardless of what their inclinations and reasoning powers makes them choose; equal status means that we must tax them all equally. Otherwise, we find that the government plays one group of people against another, with the same old results and outcomes as are found everywhere— where most income taxes are paid by the few while the many are exempted. When people object to this inequality, they blame the government for it, when in fact they should blame themselves for failing to understand the need to make rules that are universal in application. Everyone defends the tax-exempt status of their favorite nonprofits (such as schools, universities and hospitals) missing the point that they open themselves to government abuse when it plays favorites.

We accept, of course, that some individuals are not competent to generate income, due to physical or mental impairment. We should not tax children or the truly elderly, or people with disabilities. Given our obligation to promote personal integrity and give people equal opportunities, we argue that children of the poor should be subsidized while they grow up, and people with disabilities need to be subsidized throughout their lives. Regrettably, this is not done properly in most societies.

Chapter Eleven

The Rise of Property Rights in Historical Context

Their Use and Misuse

Owning property and managing assets are essential rights and responsibilities enabling us to take care of ourselves. Property is a unique human phenomenon, and so is denial of property and limitation of property uniquely human, in the sense that both are accompanied by justifications of a political or moral nature, of which humans only are capable. This also means that maintaining property and allowing wealth creation are unique human potentialities, whose dimensions we need to explore.

When property is left unregulated and instruments of violence are not used either to diminish or increase it, a ring of freedom is heard and felt by the whole community. To be sure, instruments of violence or restriction on someone's freedom—the club, the whip, the trap, or the gun, along with the men who use them or set them up—may be used to protect or manage property, as everyone knows. However, these instruments can also be used to expand property by not only securing what one owns, but by adding to it. Instruments of defense and preservation may be turned into instruments of acquisition. What these instruments do, laws backed by credible threat to someone's freedom can also achieve: They can either protect while reaffirming the owner and ownership, or they can interrupt this protection by meddling with the transfer of titles to property. This intrusion is simultaneous with the diminution and denial to someone of a something that is owned. Is property a uniquely human phenomenon? Don't birds own the nest they build? Don't beavers own the dam they assemble?

Isn't property pro-prior-ty—i.e., that thing for the sake of which the birds or beavers took *first* action toward it, established it in the first place, created it and came up with it in order to enjoy it first and foremost? Do they not defend this nest and their young as their own, even as themselves, as those beings that are first and foremost in their care?

The connection of living beings to certain aspects of the environment and the anticipated result of their actions in it are common features of all creatures of the earth. But there is another understanding that is specific to humans only: The assertion of a title, the legal standing of that title, and its possible transfer to another person. Inasmuch as persons come and go, both in physical space and in time, and inasmuch as interests and the value of some efforts change, transfers of property and assets do occur on an ongoing basis. Henceforth titles are constantly written, or rewritten, recognizing special use and enjoyment by this or that holder of the title, its new owner. We are able to define property and assets by stating that we stand for them as their beneficiaries in the first place, and we can transfer this recognition to others whereby we lose our first status. The fact that assistance or interference may occur from others between these two events, is a clear matter of concern for freedom, i.e., for humans in the care of themselves. What concerns should we have in holding property and in transferring it? Such is the twofold fundamental question we will try to answer in this chapter.

We have to grant that a few possessions of intrinsic value are not transferable: life, liberty, good fortune, knowledge, wisdom, morality, and indeed self-actualization.[1] Property, assets and liabilities can be shared, but they can also be transferred, and our freedom will be greatly enhanced by proper care being taken of these instrumental possessions. Can we separate the ownership of goods and their management? Can we be owners of essential goods without managing them, without being concerned with holding which assets and with limiting which liabilities—while they are being held and transferred?

We will consider three approaches to the above questions: (1) some simple biblical notions of an earth gifted to men so as to make it fruitful; (2) the assertions of important thinkers—from various eras, Greek, Roman, Christian and Enlightenment—on the ultimate, sovereign power of the natural rights of "We the People" (the essential "mine" and "yours"); and (3) the realization that the transformation of labor, work and action[2] into capital is a prerogative of citizens, by citizens and for citizens as individuals, which cannot be discharged upon third party bureaucratic entities. As we shall see, these three approaches are well within the kin of Western civilization—in addition we think they overlap and are mutually complementary.

The Judeo-Christian texts as well as the tradition of Natural Law (started by Aristotle, highlighted by the Stoics and Cicero, continued through the Christian Medieval thinkers and picked up by the Scottish and European

Enlightenment and Immanuel Kant) provide us with signposts and bench-marks highlighting the importance of property; they encourage a positive understanding of power by individuals and simultaneously provide barriers and restrictions on attempts by sovereigns (Pharaohs, Caesars, Potentates, Kings, Machiavellian princes) to lord their superior status upon the rest, with no care and concern for knowledge or wisdom that did not originate in themselves.

The fact that the earth was created—or just happens to be—a place of diversity derives in part from the reality of wealth being made possible on the planet by non-contiguous peoples eventually coming into contact with each other. In other words, people cannot disperse without their future offspring ever encountering each other. This condition of the earth is implicit in *Genesis*; it implies that the unfolding community of humans must learn from each other in their diversity while also respecting each other, none being free to ignore, diminish or kill the others—causing a potential waste and lessening of creation.

In the biblical narrative, the first killing takes place at the hand of Cain raging against his brother, Abel. Both had been competing for recognition by Yahweh ("I am that I am") for their work. The older, Cain was devoted to cultivating the earth, following the injunction on husbanding: "You shall tend the earth." The younger Abel would provide his services by shepherding and contributing beautiful animals from healthful flocks. Both the wanderings of the nomads, and the sedentary work of the agriculturists, were needed to fulfill the above injunction.

Yet, it is easy to see that the first-born, Cain, chose a more difficult task—labor, work and being an advocate of the commodities produced—than Abel, his brother. The shepherd moves from one pasture to another, rounds up his flock, keeps his dogs at the periphery preventing wild animals prowling nearby to attack and kill the more precious, domesticated ones. By contrast, Cain had to till the ground, plant seeds, watch the seedlings, harvest the crops, and secure them from weather, spoilage and plunder. The labor and the work seem to be greater—and taxing more manifold efforts—on Cain's side than on Abel's. Little surprise, then, that Cain expected higher recognition. When he didn't get it and Yahweh granted the younger brother the sign that the property of the well-tended flock is pleasant to this Lord of lords, the older brother took dark umbrage. And all this work of his was for nothing? Let Abel lie silent in the ditch and let the sweat and tears of the agriculturist be remembered forever!

What came to pass, however, was that there was no right for Cain to hold his brother an instrument to his own glory—that Cain's right to secure the fruit of the earth would not be exclusive of his brother's right to tend the sheep roaming back and forth from the old homestead. The property of the one is not exclusive of the property of the other. Whether or not they were competing, they each had the right to make a go of it, and let not the lesser choice of the second born be a prejudice against him or his descendants.

Any laborer, any worker, and any man acknowledging his debt to the order of nature or of creation will declare that killing a brother is an outrage from which he will find no rest. All persons mindful of this intrinsic value will subscribe to the nobility of being one's brother's keeper. The homestead and the homeland come to our attention. The homestead gets defined from signposts or fences; and the homeland from natural or artificial borders.

The homestead is property, and homelands, too, are now in the care of those groups of families who often forget how long ago it was they came to their part of the world. They have established habits of husbanding the land and trading its bounty. Although land property doesn't grow, its fruitfulness will depend on the technologies they use, the number of good hands working on it, on the busy people trading—making things better and life easier.[3] Obviously, depending on technologies used (and transports of goods and other conditions being factored in) assets will grow or dwindle, population centers will thrive or decline, and useful information properly collected and analyzed will make the difference between steady preparedness and muddled improvisation.

Assets grow or dwindle, and so does wealth, when harvests yield abundance or impose scarcity, i.e., when populations sink into poverty or migrate, and money can no longer buy desirable goods. Homestead and homeland are in the possession of families or groups, each one of them protecting individuals from the vagaries of the outside world, but also potentially keeping them captive under a Sovereign's rule. These possessions are managed by individuals who may understand or ignore the value of effort by their vassals or servants, who may deliver true justice or render it as one bestows gifts, unmindful that select privileges will be viewed as arbitrary acts of preference, causing dismay and rage when the valor and rights of some are denied.

This is why according to the story the Israelites—unimpressed by the myths of divine origin of the great pharaohs and aware of the potential for mischief by what they saw about to happen on the ground—had to step out of Egypt, into a place of their own, this land promised to them for being counted among the peoples of the earth. This is not merely a special manifest destiny for a chosen people, it is the expected and manifest destiny of men and women free to worship and go about their business as they see fit. A similar notion was not far from the minds of the Pilgrims landing at Plymouth, covenanting between themselves to remain free while relying on mutual care; all such men abiding by the promise of reciprocal altruism and trade, all free and equal under the law.

For men to be fully aware of the earth as their abode, several elements come to play an equally central part. Here we focus on three essential ones: the cosmological reality of the earth as a sphere, the understanding of the "mine" and "yours" as ultimate realities, and the keen sense that our decisions are enhanced or diminished by what others grant us or refuse to do.

As long as men didn't take seriously the limited and spherical nature of the earth, and as long as they didn't overcome their first notion of the earth as stationary and motionless, they experienced a limited sense of adventure. The corollary is that they would take only limited advantage of commerce. Only when the realization came about that the earth was a satellite of the Sun spinning on a slanted axis, did the full consequences emerge. Trading across all continents of the globe could take place and, in its wake, a true cosmopolitan outlook could develop.

Directing the human world in a proper way and sharing the earth with all took root in the Greek, Roman and Christian worlds, and owe their impetus to the ideas of natural law. The impetus originated in Aristotle's notion of human beings as political animals, endowed with speech and potentially able to understand the realities of their world in its entirety.[4] The notion developed toward the end of the Roman Republic that concerned citizens should only focus on a well-defined set of proper duties to self and others and on the notion that what's proper to each depends on circumstances. In the Roman Stoic understanding, all men are bound within a community by their capacity to be of service, which they initiate freely as benefiting them and sustaining everything else, too. Owning property, holding assets, and limiting liabilities beyond your control are all in various degrees part and parcel of being a citizen of the world. The Catholic Church in the seminal writings of the Church Fathers and Thomas Aquinas kept this fundamental teaching alive in its practice and encouragement of education, whose purpose was to promote the work of all under the guidance of the best qualified.

Freedom, as the primary condition of natural right, was enlarged and given a true cosmopolitan outreach when free trade became a stated objective of men of action in Western Europe. It had started with the Italian and Northern European trading during the Renaissance. The modern version of the spirit of enterprise—which is to be of service to self and others—owes its key formulations to the views of such essential thinkers as John Locke, Adam Smith, Montesquieu, the English Whigs and the American Founding Fathers.[5] A similar insistence on a fundamental connection of the self with others and a shared stewardship of the earth is present in all their essential views and writings. Immanuel Kant focused on the inalienable binding of each and every man to a primordial "mine," which has a correlate of a primordial "yours" that cannot fail to exist and must be recognized. The historical realities of slavery or manorial bondage (serfdom) were made unjustifiable in the enlightened version of natural rights. You cannot make another your own, nor can another own you. When a person is not free, one should endeavor to make him free, for the good of everyone.

Being centered on self and being interested in the world at large are not incompatible concerns. In the world of the Enlightenment the realities of mutual altruism are in full display. Someone cannot make a gift unless he has something to hold in his own right. The gift transfer inevitably brings the individual into the mutually beneficial altruistic mode of thinking. What another accepts now as a gift, prior to anyone making such a claim, is his because the original someone transferred his earlier right and title to the second person—a transfer that both individuals expect others to fully recognize and honor as legitimate.

A similar agreeable freedom is also on display when people trade goods of all kinds. One's possessing a certain good through natural right, merely validated by statutory law, is what enabled another—in the case of trading—to claim it rightfully and lawfully his, while no one else has the right to step up in front of him and deprive the new owner of his possession. Prior freedom of use and enjoyment (the natural right of all men to own a share of the world through their labor, work and service) is the elementary basis upon which bartering/trading is possible. Bartering and trading involve a mutual transfer of things along with the transfer of rights of usage and enjoyment.

We have now decisively moved into the realm of the potentially endless decisions we make in our lives: willing this, refusing that, avoiding, preferring, ranking, owning, discarding—which all add up to trading, and selling things or services that are relevant to our enjoyment of the earth and our self-actualization. We see ourselves fully in charge of decisions that affect us in the realm of action: we are connected to each other by labor, work, and service—and not by enjoyments of the contemplative lifestyle, that of the hermit thinker or the saint. Having possessions and properties—managing and trading assets—these realities are at the core of taking charge and taking care of ourselves.

How can it all go wrong? And if it does, how can what went wrong be brought back on the right track again? We have already seen that the great luminaries of freedom, John Locke, Adam Smith, and Immanuel Kant along with the American Founding Fathers expected, even heralded, a new age of freedom once the powers-that-be are restrained from intruding upon the natural rights of citizens claiming what is rightfully theirs. Yet, something has gone wrong in modern times, starting in the 19th century. The concern for the natural rights of all individuals has been replaced by the management of all affairs by third-party bureaucrats for the benefit of sliced and segmented social groups. Has the time come to backtrack on natural rights and hold back on freedom, or should we reassert freedom by restraining restrictions on, and by controlling, the bureaucrats' vaunted independence and so-called expertise?

The 19th century brought with it both industrialization and colonization, with the latter degenerating into imperialism. A massive intrusion of despotism occurred when the imperial powers of Europe held the world captive to the interests of one class of its populace, and when they justified their clamp on others abroad with racist theories of supremacy. European powers slid into militarism, the imposition of colonial control abroad, and the use of race thinking as a justification for their actions. These trends tarnished the ring of freedom and elevated its opposite: Control and dependency for many of the people under their "protection."

We should look on the wheelers and dealers of the modern colonial era. Internally, industrial growth occurred and new industrial benefits were soon apparent to the European populations. Externally, in dealing with the non-industrial world, these wheelers and dealers pushed in every way possible their governments to step where independent nations should have never gone. Those wheelers and dealers wanted fast returns on their investments in virgin lands, and they forced the hand of the state to guarantee their gambles. While this happened, the concerned citizens of the richer countries didn't step up forcefully to sound the alarm on the whip of militarism dominating their world, among other dangers.[6]

Continents or near continents—Africa, India, large swaths of Asia—as well as individual countries in those territories were dominated in just a few years. Subjection was termed "protection" and outright domination received the euphemism of "assistance" on the way to reaching the pinnacle of civilization. The real estate of the Imperialistic powers of Europe (England, France, Germany, Russia), and even the United States (permanently in Hawaii and only tentatively in the Philippines and parts of Mexico) increased greatly in the decades prior to the First World War. Yet, imperialistic real estate wouldn't translate into greater wealth, a safer holding of assets, and the limiting of liabilities.

Two tools—bureaucratic and militaristic outreach—were the means of imperialist domination, whose costs and liabilities turned impossible to limit and discharge with the profits of colonialism. Imperialistic and bureaucratic costs grew enormously because of the unavoidable growth and upkeep of their unwilling subjects, who also revolted every time they could. Also growing was the cost of militarism on account of both its internal, domestic requirements and the pressure from threatening competitors.

The intrusion of imperialist and racist statutory laws affected the global natural rights of people all around the world and their ability to rise on their own. This was waste on global scale, which did not accrue to the benefit of the wheelers and dealers. Its early opponents, the Englishman Richard Cobden and the Frenchman Frédéric Bastiat anticipated the failure of imperialism, in the 1840's and into the 1850's. The same waste was anticipated and turned into argument of hot resentment by Marx and Lenin, predicting that bourgeois sovereignty would collapse under the costly contradiction of its practices.

The theoretician and practitioner of active socialism argued that preventing laborers and workers from converting their work into capital couldn't be sustained—and that a contradiction existed for the bourgeois class of the entrepreneurs—formerly seeking "free trade," yet now clamoring for protection from the State. The cost of this collapse and contradiction was two World Wars, not to mention a series of socialist revolutions, all aiming at guaranteeing and spreading the wealth; all ending in diminishing it everywhere.

The rise of those multinational concerns was made possible by large national and cross-national investments, and it brought about a divorce between ownership and control (formerly the affair of families or individuals) of business enterprises. When management has gained the upper hand, it has been more than willing to form alliances with the state, giving rise to the capacity for seizing and holding lands and peoples. The old meaning of control—as in self-control and discipline, those virtues of the Greek, Roman, Christian and Early Modern worlds—were thrown overboard. Control has become, in both the imperialist phase of the Western World and now in the post-imperialist phase, control of the state, by the state, for the state, in collusion with Big Business and Big Labor.

Unchecked control by the state reaches all aspects of personal life, managing individuals in all areas of social, educational, health, financial, and even recreational life. Although the State's social engineers do not directly control business's day-to-day operations, bureaucrats and politicians try to do so through regulation. This situation was more obvious during the imperialist phase of the 19th and early 20th centuries, when European investors demanded that their sovereign states protect and defend their investments abroad. The same happened when the United States invaded various countries in the Caribbean in the first half of the 20th century. Control over property, possessions, and all types of assets shifted dramatically when the self-restraint and risk-taking of the individual, by the individual, for the individual was replaced by the risk-taking of the managers, who counted on the nation to shift the burden of their gambles (and liabilities) on to taxpayers, who had to pay for state interventions in other countries.

While the chartered privileges of colonial companies now seem a thing of the past, protectionism of a new kind has been borne: the entitlement culture, which has grown into the supreme credo of the day. Control by the state of unchecked "independent agencies" (such as Freddie Mac and Fannie Mae) extended to elite managers the power to make decisions over new aspects of economic life. Control is no longer in the care of the concerned, risk-taking individual. Control in the entitlement culture is encouraged by those forces seeking to produce more areas of regulation for the sake of guaranteeing success to the favorites of the government.

The solution to this predicament can only be that—since taxpayers on the way to extinction will not accept their impending demise—concerned citizens will have to reinstate forms of legislation that favor property, ownership, assets control and the limiting of liabilities (including the Federal Debt). Managers will not manage properties and assets without participating in the losses they incur—through bad luck or bad judgment.

A world held together by cosmopolitan reciprocities and intercontinental travel will also be a world held together by accountability to self and others. The early Greek, Roman, Christian and early modern traditions had insisted on an ethos of communication with self-control and discipline at the root of a lifestyle of limited personal liberality (generosity), going hand in hand with courage and justice.

In conclusion, we hope that this perspective offers a multilayered but complementary series of arguments and of time-tested incentives for increasing our human capital of intelligence and mutual assistance, which must never be overruled—controlled or prevented—by any government or sectarian practice whatsoever—be it Non-Governmental Organizations that benefit from the generosity of private donors but are immune from risk-taking and weigh on political institutions while not partaking in an open process.

NOTES

1. This point is essential to ethical theories that draw their inspiration from Aristotle's focus on virtue and character. See Alasdair MacIntyre, *After Virtue: A Study in Moral Theory*, 3^d ed. (Notre Dame, Indiana: University of Notre Dame Press, 2007).

2. This threefold distinction is borrowed from Hannah Arendt's *The Human Condition*, (*Chicago*: The University of Chicago Press, 1958). She owes it to John Locke, but uses it to untangle and expose the reversal of values that have characterized the modern world's demotion of thinking and elevation of acting—all the while diminishing the political virtues that flourish in the public realm.

3. This point is implicit in the Bible. It is also explicit in Hesiod's account of what current humanity is saddled with. We must not take our eyes away from the realities of the Iron Age, which expanded the abilities of the many and empowered them to higher accomplishments. See Hesiod's *Works and Days*, trans. Hugh Evelyn White, accessed October 20, 2015, http://www.sacred-texts.com/cla/hesiod/works.htm.

4. On this account it makes sense for educators to highlight that Western culture owes its reach across the globe to philosophy, whose full-fledged development came to fruition in Athens and in Greece in general. The subsequent addition of Jerusalem confirmed morality as an aspect not merely of a well-structured state but of human beings in general. Rome's addition—from the point of view of the humanities—is limited to the Republic, the critics of the Empire, and to the Latin language, the *lingua franca* of the medieval world.

5. See especially Daniel Hannan, *Inventing Freedom, How the English-Speaking Peoples Made the Modern World* (New York: HarperCollins Publishers, 2013).

6. See Murray N. Rothbard, *Classical Economics, An Austrian Perspective on the History of Economic Thought*, vol. 2 (Auburn, Alabama: Ludwig von Mises Institute, 2006).

Chapter Twelve

Bringing Back Legitimacy to Government

In previous chapters we have argued not just for the need to reform the legal structure in this country, but also for the renewal of the moral values that currently prevail in the United States. We have argued, for example, for limiting the scope of government and changing inheritance laws; we have called for the creation of private groups that could help to limit the practice of abortion by means of financial incentives; we want to increase the use of private insurance to lift the tax burden on those who do not practice risky activities, and so on. But these changes cannot come about unless the population looks at our national problems from a different perspective, which emphasizes self-actualization and the acceptance of personal duties towards others.

Wanting or proposing change is not enough. Others have tried and have failed, to some extent. What, then, can we learn from social movements, and how much can we expect when we go through the constitutional route of changing the nation by means of constitutional amendments? These are the two main questions that we address in this chapter.

Social movements do have an impact on the political life of the country, but oftentimes they concentrate on limited goals and confuse symptoms with the diseases that afflict us. We will pay attention to three important social movements in the United States: The Tea Party, Occupy Wall Street, and the Ferguson protests, which have spawned the Black Lives Matter movement. Each of these movements now presents a different stage of development, and as a result, we can all learn something from their growth.

Some have argued that the Tea Party movement originated with Congressman Ron Paul's presidential campaign of 2007, when he received a substantial amount of money (originating in small donations) on the anniversary of the Boston Tea Party. However, Ron Paul was an established Libertarian candidate whose views on foreign policy were not in accord with the rank and file of the Republican Party. Yet his money-raising achievement and his ability to energize young people for his campaign demonstrated to Republican activists that they could invigorate conservative members of the Republican party and demand government reform with a view to limiting the size of the government sector—especially the federal government. Since then the Tea Party movement has supported—and been instrumental in—the election of various candidates for the Republican Party, including Scott Brown in Massachusetts, Ted Cruz in Texas and Rand Paul in Kentucky (the son of then Congressman Ron Paul). Today the movement is large enough to be fused and at odds, simultaneously, with the Republican Party regarding most issues—with the exception of immigration.

The Tea Party movement faced serious obstacles in its development. Whereas the Libertarian Party had been based on specific moral principles (defending the rights of people to be left alone with regard to their personal behavior, and insisting that the federal government should not interfere in the behaviors and actions of other governments overseas, so as to avoid military interventions and war), the Tea Party ignored all references to social and moral issues, and concentrated almost exclusively on limiting the scope of government. This position attracted Republican Party activists, who felt that the distinction between the two major parties was rapidly eroding. By having a single focus, the Tea Party was avoiding the pitfall of the Republican Party, that had previously been damaged in elections where its candidates were closely associated with pro-life positions and anti-gay rights pronouncements. The Tea Party banner became a simple one: "We want limited government."

The problem, of course, with one-issue movements is that they are unable to create a coalition of interest groups, and in fact their emphasis on a single issue becomes really threatening to those on the other side of the issue. For example, Libertarians became a threat to many conservative Republicans on social issues, and the Tea Party movement became a threat to minority groups who received huge subsidies through the government, including public education, food stamps or their equivalent, housing subsidies, etc. Hence, while the Tea Party was not a racist organization, it turned out that few minorities joined it because it was not in their economic interest to limit government largesse. The press, in turn, used the lack of participation of minorities within the movement to launch false accusations of racism against the movement, creating a racial conflict where there was none, other than diverging economic interests.

We have argued in this book that economic dependence is both ultimately and strikingly inimical to the long-term interest of the poor and all minority groups. However, as long as the economic pie keeps increasing as a result of technical change, trade, specialization and the protection of property rights, it will always be possible for the government (and those who work for and benefit from it) to take income from the most productive members of society and use it both to placate and woo into further grievances the poorer members of society. This engenders a culture of dependency and festering irritation that is bound to create a greater divide between those who have acquired human capital and those who have not. The conflict between the haves and the have-nots has gotten worse over time, and there is no end in sight to the divide.

The Occupy Wall Street Movement, whose main point of contention is precisely growing income inequality and the undue influence of corporate giants on governments, has recently exploited this divide. It would be unwise and unrealistic to argue that the Occupy Movement does not have a point because income inequality has in fact risen in recent years, and the firms in the financial system (not necessarily all corporations) have become quite dependent upon the government—in particular the Federal Reserve Bank and the Treasury—for their economic wellbeing. Most regrettably, the financial system has followed the lead set for it by the government and therefore been participant in the entire exercise of plutocratic rent seeking. In tandem, the financial system and the government have produced huge misallocation of resources by (a) maintaining interest rates artificially low; (b) accommodating the gigantic borrowing needs of the federal government (which will not balance its budget); and (c) eroding financial stability by forcing banks and other financial institutions to lend funds to people and groups who do not have the potential of repaying those funds (as it was made clear by the collapse of the housing market in recent years). Meanwhile, industrial firms in America fall off the financial cliff as the government continues to maintain the value of the dollar artificially high (keeping artificially cheap imports coming in) and imposes upon them suicidal restrictions and regulations that do not bear upon their competitors abroad.

The pathologies are well-known: the lack of industrial jobs, the culture of dependency that has been created in America, the creation of minority ghettos of huge proportions within American cities, the acceptance of dysfunctional schools and dysfunctional families, and worst of all, the lack of significant employment opportunities for the poorly educated, resulting from subsidized technical changes and federal intrusion in labor markets. The crime rates in minority ghettos is unnerving to anyone who happens to become acquainted with them. Therefore, it is absolutely not surprising that police forces (whose members now belong to all ethnic and racial backgrounds) find themselves oftentimes unable to maintain order except by means of excessive force and intimidation. This has finally exploded in the flashpoint of the Ferguson riots and national protests against racial profiling and outbursts against police brutality. The widespread resentment towards police forces in minority communities cannot be denied, and it is the focal point for the Black Lives Matter movement.

Governor Bobby Jindal of Louisiana famously said that the Republican Party has to stop being the stupid party. Let us emphasize and illustrate this point. So far, the most important venues facing social unrest and social turmoil occur in places where Democrats have been in charge for long periods of time: California, New York, Illinois, and the District of Columbia. Why don't Republicans point this out? Even Missouri, where the Ferguson riots originated, is and has been in control of the Democratic Party for several years. Florida, where riots have also occurred, is no longer a Democratic stronghold, yet the impact of Democratic policies on housing and urban discrimination is widely felt in the state. To these examples we must add the fact that Democratic machines have controlled most American major cities and guided the political and social lives of their citizens. These machines have destroyed the viability of many cities, with Detroit being the saddest and most telling example of such a process of disintegration and decay.

Republicans, in turn, flee to the suburbs, where they are able to ignore the suffering of the poor. In Florida, which is now controlled by Republicans, the party does nothing to end the extreme segregation that exists in so many cities. We have to realize, then, that while greater income inequality exists (as a result of poor public education and the lack of an industrial structure), and while excessive force has become part and parcel of policing practices (despite the goodwill of those police forces and their efforts to avoid falling into this trap), we need to understand and address the root causes of these conditions, and not gloss over—without offering any permanent solution to—the symptoms that they give rise to.

If we were heading a social movement, these are the goals that we would propose. First, we need to change the moral foundation for our beliefs. Therefore, we need to provide guidance on how to live the life of a good person in the private sector and in the wider world, where real opportunities should be present but are often denied to many citizens. In other words, we need to give people a set of moral intuitions that provide guidance on how they should behave within families, in the business sector, and in our schools. With regard to schools, some will highlight a rosy scenario and claim that our progressive schools put up a fight against sexism, racism, xenophobia, etc. That response—in light of the evident decline of a nation increasingly at risk of educational collapse—demonstrates the hollowness and incompetence of those who make such assertions. The issue is not to be against this or that "ism;" the issue is to give the ethical *foundations* for combating sexism, racism, xenophobia, etc.

Here the observation is stark: Our schools do not teach moral values. What they do is simply indoctrinate students into doing (or saying) this or that, or not doing (or not saying) this third, fourth or fifth thing. There is not an ethical education at work. What the educational system has morphed into is a mixture, or smorgasbord, of Pavlovian indoctrination protocols. Outside the controlled environment targeting laboratory rats, indeed forms of cooperation and "live and let live" norms (in combination with "you may fail and others may just fail, too") do take place. And so, just like the laboratory-learned responses fail to describe what goes on in the real animal world, likewise in the human world of 2015 American education, indoctrination fails when students are faced with economic interests which move them one way or another. Students are confused by the discovery of how irrelevant some of their schooling has been. No wonder so many concerned parents choose homeschooling for their offspring. We aim to make our students complacent in a shallow way, rather than giving them the foundations to become moral citizens.

In the old days, of course, our morals were based on biblical teaching, but since that is no longer acceptable in academic discourse, we need to reintroduce into our curriculum well established and coherent systems of ethics. To do that we need to talk about, and discuss such authors as Epictetus, Aristotle and Kant, among others. When biblical norms are thrown out the window, great ethical thinkers must be rushed into the classroom.

Due to faulty exposure to American history and its grounding in Western thinking, too many of our teachers are inept, and show themselves both profoundly ignorant and deeply ill-at-ease when it comes to arguing ethical norms. Many have no clue, or only have insignificant clues, about the great force of the classical (Greek, English, French) tragedies or comedies, they have been fundamentally hampered by the "bigotry of low expectations." Too often they simply cannot show their students the vitality of the humanities—English, American, French, German, Italian and Spanish humanities, which promote a broad mentality of critical thinking in the midst of challenging circumstances. Only a handful (if that!) of students graduating from the average American high school in 2015 have heard about Don Quixote, or Dante's love for Beatrice, or the pleasing fables of La Fontaine or the hard-hitting critique of French society by Molière. And equally vast majorities have no clue as to who the great English poets are, let alone why Mark Twain's writings present such an important counterpoint to the counterfeit and bogus climate of his times, or to whom and why Martin Luther King, Jr. wrote his "Letter from a Birmingham Jail."

In addition, students are never taught that governments are never, ever, the source of our freedoms. Better governments always arose as a result of people demanding and obtaining restrictions on the powers of governments. Even our Founding Fathers, whom we greatly admire as intellectual giants, could not come up with a practical and ideal government that would last for long; for as soon as such a government was instituted, special interest became dominant and many injustices (including slavery—and after the Civil

War the disaster of Reconstruction) were justified. Hence our true goal has to be to limit the powers of government—rather than thinking in utopian fashion that government is the solution to our social and economic problems. America learned this painful lesson many times, but especially in the War to End All Wars (the First World War), which resulted in the rise of Hitler and Stalin, two of the most evil men the world has ever seen.

Market institutions allow for competition and change, and no better institutional arrangement has yet been found to promote human welfare. These institutions have defects, which include lack of full information, the existence of natural monopolies and the constant disruption of market forces by the bureaucracy, but these are corrected naturally over the long term. Regrettably, markets are severely impacted by dramatic technological changes every so often, and these changes alter the bargaining power of players in those markets. However, these breaks are absorbed over time, and new competitors arise in the long run. Those of us who have lived long enough remember the false prophets of the 1960s telling us that General Motors would dictate the path of American industry and culture for centuries to come; yet that firm is now a weak giant rescued from bankruptcy by the current Administration. Even Bill Gates may turn into an unknown to future generations. Ideas remain (that is why we still remember those who came up with new ideas) but simply successful men and women are footnotes to history.

We have the tools to build a new social movement in this country, because we hold powerful ideas to do so, but this social movement would face the same problems that other social movements have faced in the recent past; namely, the institutional structures that they threaten: political parties, economic interests, educational bureaucracies and entrenched politicians, of both parties. The best that we can hope to do is educate people regarding the problems that they face (including their own lack of moral foundations and proclivities), and the legal options that could slowly bring about change. For that reason, we now turn to constitutional amendments and how they come about.

We have had 27 amendments to our Constitution, ten of which (making up the Bill of Rights) were part and parcel of the original constitutional process, being adopted within three years after the Constitution itself went into effect. Article 5 of the Constitution allows Congress, or a national convention assembled at the request of the state legislatures, to propose constitutional amendments. So far, amendments have only originated with Congress, although it is true that in the past some state legislatures have voted in favor of calling forth a national convention as a way of forcing Congress into proposing specific amendments. But no national convention called by the states has ever been assembled.

Once Congress proposes an amendment (usually by means of a joint resolution which must pass with two thirds of the votes in each chamber), it is sent to the state legislatures, which must approve the amendment; three fourths of the state legislatures must approve the amendment for it to become part of the Constitution. However, an amendment sent to the states for approval may also gain approval by means of votes in state conventions. So far only one amendment, the 21st, which repealed Prohibition, has ever been approved in this fashion. Congress may or may not set a deadline for the approval of an amendment by the states. The last amendment to the Constitution, ratified in 1992, took 202 years, 7 months and 12 days before its ratification! (It states that changes to the salary of members of Congress cannot go into effect until the following congressional session.) Congress has used the amendment process to deal with trying political circumstances (such as abolishing slavery or prohibiting the denial of the right to vote), to respond to social movements (prohibiting and then later allowing for the "transportation for delivery or use" of alcohol), to define or extend the rights of citizenship, to make changes in the electoral process, and to deal with succession issues. Generally speaking, Constitutional changes are extremely difficult to bring about.

Finally, since the country has grown dramatically over the course of its more than two-hundred-year history, and technological change has given rise to deep structural changes that have changed both institutions and beliefs, we assert that constitutional change has occurred surreptitiously or indirectly, by means of novel and ever changing Supreme Court decisions. We make this assertion with full confidence that we can demonstrate this point. At one time, for instance, the Supreme Court was in full accord with the establishment of religion at the state level; yet decades later this view was rejected. At another point, the right to unionize labor was interpreted as the creation of monopoly power; yet decades later this same view was abandoned and labor gained monopoly power. The Supreme Court once accepted equal but separate schools, but then it rejected them. The list goes on and on, and it is worth emphasizing that these changes were totally independent of the amendment process. In other words, existing amendments (especially those in the Bill of Rights, but also the 14th amendment) gave rise to evolving interpretations of our Constitution.

Liberals contend, based upon the above historical record, that the US Constitution is a "living document" that is subject to new and novel interpretations by the Supreme Court. That has been indeed true in practice, but such practice is not formally incorporated in anything written within the Constitution. That was not the intention of the Founding Fathers of this country.

Conservatives, of course, do not deny the legitimacy of the amendment process, but they certainly deny many of the novel interpretations that the Supreme Court has made in order to interpret the Constitution. In retrospect, one can voice that, at various times, Liberals have felt the same way, when they did not like Supreme Court decisions—even in recent times. The root of the problem is deciding, today and now, what the Constitution really means.

Such being the case, it is obvious that a new Constitutional convention is in order. Yet everyone is afraid of one because there is the fear of what a Constitutional convention might bring. To obviate that fear, or at the very least allay it, we need to find an anchor to the rule of law while the Constitutional convention does its work.

It is for this reason that we make the following proposal. State legislatures need to re-ratify the US Constitution, including all of its approved amendments. However, this ratification process should also call for a national convention once two thirds of the states follow a similar step. Such a call for a national convention must specify that the convention's stated purpose is to evaluate which Supreme Court decisions can be interpreted as either in violation of the provisions of the amended (and re-ratified) Constitution, or as necessary improvements of the amended (and re-ratified) Constitution.

The convention should then come up with a list of short constitutional amendments that would invalidate Supreme Court decisions or that would explicitly confirm those decisions required to keep up with modern times, even when they contradict the amended (and re-ratified) Constitution. Each of these amendments would then be sent to the state legislatures for approval or rejection. This is the only decisive way we can decide what our Constitution really means! It is perhaps the only institutional means that is at our disposals—one strongly wished for by Thomas Jefferson—to make the American experiment in self-government relevant to our times, a time that certainly experiences the "urgency of now."

The main goal of the process is to legitimize the ground rules under which we live. We neither support nor reject Conservative or Liberal ideologies. Our goal is to update the Constitution, and place "We the People," or at the very least our representatives, in charge of the government we live in. There is no doubt that Supreme Court decisions have dramatically altered the Constitutional foundations under which we live; the time has come to go back to our foundations and reject or affirm prior Supreme Court decisions. In Jeffersonian fashion, but also in the fashion of the Civil Rights Activists, we need to assert that we have a role to play in deciding which ground rules need to apply to the governing process.

We do not doubt, for example, that such a constitutional convention would reaffirm the rights of children to receive equal education within a racially integrated environment; but we also suspect that such a convention would take seriously the tenth amendment and not allow the federal government to have a free reign in dictating curricular matters to the states. There is a major difference between the rights of children as future citizens of individual states versus the expanding role of a federal bureaucracy that wants to tell every state what to do.

The thought of a constitutional convention brings up fears into the minds of both Liberals and Conservatives. What they fail to appreciate is that our greatest fear must be the delegitimization of government within our country. We do not know anymore what our Constitution stands for, and we have the right to know. Once we do that, we can move on to some constitutional amendments that we would like to see added to our Constitution; these are the subject of our next chapter.

Chapter Thirteen

Proposed Legal and Constitutional Changes

Changing people's minds to the viewpoint we propose should occur before changing the legal structure in which they live. That is the reason for writing this book. But let us suppose, for the sake of argument, that we have been able to convince people to adopt this new perspective. This would mean that they have accepted our plea for more limited government, and the need for institutional structures (including greater use of market competition and insurance programs) that internalize the moral values that we advocate. People would then not think about achieving peer acceptance but of achieving self-actualization and accepting greater responsibility for the welfare of others. Let us then consider the following legal and constitutional changes that we propose.

Schools, for example, would become legally bound to discover the wide range of natural talents that students possess, and would assign diverse curricula that would enhance a variety of talents. The age of a standard curriculum for everyone would be gone forever, while the success of teachers would be objectively measured in terms of the progress that individual students make in developing their special skills. Parents would be held responsible for the academic and practical potential of their children, and would be urged neither to impose excessive nor restrained demands on their children. The school goals would not be to achieve the shallow "happiness" of children, but rather the far more realistic approach to enhance their development, which would yield, if not happiness, at least greater contentment and satisfaction among the children. They would be treated as ends and not means to achieve either extraordinary or unimpressive results.

It is, then, within this context that we want to propose a series of Constitutional amendments that, as far as we know, have never been proposed in the past. We begin by noting that in the same way we think of an optimal education for children, we should think of an optimal size for states. There is no reason to believe that the boundaries of our states should be determined by historical events. To make a persuasive case, let us consider some dysfunctional boundary examples, far away from our emotions, which are easy to find in Africa.

Take Nigeria as a case in point. Nigeria is the most populous country in Africa, with approximately 180 million people. Over 250 different ethnic groups inhabit the country, but four of them are dominant: The Hausa, the Igbo, the Yoruba and the Fulani. The country is torn apart by religious divisions, with the Muslims controlling the North and the Christians controlling the South. There are at least four major languages, and hundreds of minor languages and dialects; it is for this reason that English has been made the official language of the country. It is no wonder that the country experienced one deadly civil war in the 1960s that led to the deaths of between one and three million people.

The diversity that one finds in Nigeria cannot be compared to the diversity that one finds in any single state of the American Union. But it is sometimes necessary to present an extreme example to drive a point; namely, that the extraordinary diversity of Nigeria makes it nearly impossible to reach a political consensus within the state. A similar situation occurs, but to a lesser degree, within American states, not just because of ethnic divisions (which are becoming more significant) but also because of economic interests. If we are going to divest greater political power into the hands of the state and local governments, such entities must be as homogeneous as possible, for otherwise the bitter divisions which we observe at the national level will be reproduced at the state and local levels. Hence we propose, first, to create a national commission that would make recommendations on how the states could or should be partitioned or rejoined into various political entities, and give the state legislatures the opportunity to recreate themselves. This commission would also suggest the creation of regional political entities with similar cultural and economic interests. The achievement of such reconfigurations would require an amendment to the Constitution. Megacities with similar cultural and economic interests could be designated as independent states; and the same would hold for megacities that somehow enjoy and thrive on cultural and economic diversity.

This State Reassignment Amendment should be viewed as taking into account the intuition behind Madison's Federalist Paper #10 in a modern context, where power needs to be reassigned and divested to geographical, business and other interest groups. It is clearly in line with the Tenth Amendment to the U.S. Constitution. We also intend this amendment to be seen, and understood, as a way to mitigate, and perhaps even redress, the legacy of the catastrophe called Reconstruction, and the raw deal that was given to many of the former slaves, not to mention the poor whites who came to detest an armed government in the Southern States—all the while preparing a segment of that white population for rent-seeking and special privileges.

Most Americans hold strong consensual views on privacy and our involvement in foreign wars. Hence privacy needs to be protected at all costs, or else the federal, and even the state governments, will know so much about the private lives of individuals that governments, at any level, will be able to manipulate the behavior of people. We need a Constitutional amendment that protects our freedoms, and all surveillance programs must come to an end—at least against those who have no serious criminal records. We advocate for a Freedom from Surveillance Amendment. Neither the government nor the private sector has a right to keep track of our private decisions. If firms lose business as a result of our insistence on keeping our privacy, so be it. Our freedom is far more important than the efficacy of anti-terrorist programs and/or marketing schemes in the private sector. It is often ignored that anti-terror programs can be most successful when not allowing immigrants and refugees into this country who do not share our cultural values.

The history of the 20th century, and the first fifteen years into the new century, have been characterized by American military involvement, or at the very least clandestine involvement, in the quarrels of Europe, Asia, Africa and Latin America. While the Second World War can be justified on both moral and national security grounds, most other wars involved the deception of the American people by our own government. There is a big difference between achieving superior military strength, which is quite desirable, and engaging militarily in other people's businesses. We do not have friends; we have compelling national security interests that demand the maintenance of superior military might. This does not mean that we may not, or should not, support regimes that are actually friendly to us; but it means that those alliances must be made on the basis of national security interests and the convergence of military strategies. Therefore, we advocate a National Security Amendment not only requiring strict approval by Congress for any type of military intervention lasting longer than three months, but that declares in no uncertain terms that American national security (and nothing else) will determine our military alliance with other nations.

In recent times, immigration has become a serious and divisive issue within our country. In our opinion, the influx of a large number of illegal immigrants (especially from our Southern border) has taken place for a reason; namely, that the federal government wanted to balance the growing economic and political power of the black population within the United States. Blacks could no longer be kept as second class citizens after their participation in the Second World War and the Korean War—a time when discrimination was so blatant and repugnant that black involvement in those wars was achieved by the creation of fighting units made up of people of different races. It is not surprising at all that the Civil Rights Movement took place after black Americans shed their blood for this country, and started thinking of their war participation in terms of a promise for racial equality. If the black population could fight in theaters of war abroad, they could equally fight in theaters of contention at home, demanding their political rights. [1]

Such was the idea behind Martin Luther King, Jr.'s evocation of the U.S. Constitution as a "promissory note." While European immigration after the Second World War would have weakened the economic position of Anglo Americans, Latino immigrants, especially from Mexico, would compete with blacks for jobs at the lower levels of the economic ladder. Hence it made sense, after the racial riots of the 1960s and 1970s to allow not thousands or hundreds of thousands, but in actuality millions of poor Latinos into this country. This massive transfer of (disempowered) labor was done with the full cooperation and collusion of various agencies in the Administrative branch of government. Large increases in legal immigration would not have passed Congress.

This illegal immigration surreptitiously pushed by government entities over decades has transformed the demographic, cultural and political land-scape of our country. Since the American West and Southwest, plus Florida, had a long history of Spanish traditions and cultural norms, the Latino popu-lation increases have been managed reasonably well until recent times, when Latinos have moved in large number to other regions within the United States. The clash of cultures has been reaching a boiling point, with good reason, as we explain below.

Suppose that Mexico had twenty million illegal immigrants composed almost entirely of Anglo Americans. Would it not be the case that the demo-graphic, cultural and political landscape of Mexico stood to be dramatically transformed, making Mexico a far more diverse and conflicted society than it already is, with far more economic inequality that existed there endemically prior to the intrusion? Mexico would not, of course, tolerate such an illegal Anglo American population; in fact, it does not even tolerate much smaller illegal groups from Central America or the Caribbean!

The issue of (mainly Latino) illegal immigration to America needs to be understood, with all of its ramifications. Spanish is a world language, like English, and it does not present the great challenge that minor languages present elsewhere in Africa and other continents; its diffusion in our country is no more a threat than the diffusion of French in Canada. Furthermore, it is in the interest of the United States to keep friendly relations with both Mexi-co and Canada, our two closest neighbors. However, illegal Latino immigra-tion is not in the economic interest of the black population, or even in the economic interest of the Puerto Rican population, made up entirely of United States citizens. It is therefore important that we come up with a reasonable Constitutional amendment that would diminish, rather than increase, the distrust between Mexico and the United States. We propose to call this the Reciprocity Amendment.

Such an amendment would proclaim that no more citizens of another country would be accepted into the United States as legal immigrants unless a similar number of native-born American are granted citizenship rights within those countries—whether they use those rights or not. These rights of dual citizenship would be helpful to reorient the debates within Latin America towards growth and development, as well as limited government. Some readers may be surprised to learn that many leaders in Latin America (including the first President of Cuba) were United States citizens. (Can the readers name the first Indian-American Vice President of the United States, who held office in the 20th century?)[2]

If immigration is good for America (which it is), it should be good and equally desirable for other countries. Recall that we want to treat others as we would like others to treat us. The Reciprocity Amendment captures that behavioral norm—very much in line with the intuition by John Quincy Adams, who protected republican governments South of the border from European intervention. Once we sign a bilateral agreement that twenty million native-born Americans should be allowed to hold Mexican citizenship, with full voting rights, then and only then would we continue to encourage Mexican immigration into this country on a quid pro quo basis. And the same rule should apply to people from other countries, in particular Haitians, Jamaicans, Dominicans and Cubans. Glorious days of the American Republic are yet to come—something that shouldn't, and wouldn't, be surprising to the likes of Thomas Paine, Thomas Jefferson or John Quincy Adams. Our dual citizens will help create democratic governments in all of these countries. Let us encourage American migration abroad, and embrace good-neighbor policies with all our adjacent neighbors.

We propose another amendment, which we will label the Spreading Columbia Westward Amendment. To do so, we need to discuss briefly one section of the US Constitution. Article 1, section 8 reads in part: "To exercise exclusive Legislation in all cases whatsoever, over such district (not exceeding ten Miles square) as may, by Cession of particular States, and the Acceptance of Congress, become the Seat of the Government of the United States . . ." This made possible the establishment of the District of Columbia, with land donated by both Virginia and Maryland. However, it is important to note that what is now Alexandria, VA was returned to that state in 1846, and the rest of the land donated by the same state was returned in full later that year. Hence it stands to reason that a large part of District lands can be returned to Maryland. We do note, in advance of possible objections, that there is a historical precedent for doing exactly that.

In 1790 Congress decided that a ten-mile square area was not sufficient land for the seat of government, accepting donations from Maryland and

Virginia of 100 square miles. In 1846, when some of the lands were returned to Virginia, the district retained 61.4 square miles of land and 6.9 square miles of water surface. It should be obvious to even the loosest interpreters of the Constitution that the exact wording in that document was simply ignored. Since we propose subdividing the District of Columbia, it is also necessary to note that all coastal states include islands as parts of those states, and that two states in particular (Washington and Minnesota) include small non-island sections that are separated from the rest of their mainland components. The point is that no state requires land *continuity* to remain a single entity.

Therefore, the District of Columbia does not need to be contiguous, and a large part of the land donated by Maryland can be returned to that state. We propose a Constitutional amendment that would split the federal district into three non-contiguous areas, each housing one of the three branches of government: the Legislative branch made up of Congress (the House of Representatives and the Senate), the Administrative branch made up of the White House and the federal agencies, and the Judicial branch made up of the Supreme Court. While it would be easiest to keep the largest branch (the Administrative one) in the federal district, we have serious misgivings with that approach, because most buildings making up that branch are architectural eyesores and ecological dinosaurs which are extremely costly to maintain. Furthermore, the people of this great nation should have equal access to the White House, which needs to be relocated (or rebuilt) somewhere in the center of the country. Although the state of Kansas comes to mind, various states bordering Kansas could donate lands if appropriate, and they could all share in the Westward relocation of the District of Columbia. The bureaucracy could be moved gradually to its new location, after new energy-efficient buildings are completed.

We propose, then, a very small area for the federal district on the East Coast, encompassing Congress and the museums around the National Mall. All other lands of the federal district should be returned to Maryland, thereby empowering the large black population there to participate in federal elections. The White House (a term which may be offensive to people of color, to be ironically correct) can be reconstructed in Kansas, or alongside bordering states; it might be called by a different name, such as the "Presidential Term Residence," with architectural design aimed at minimizing any palatial or imperial look, and giving it no more than not-too-grand upper middle class appearance. What Brazil did with the relocation of its capital to Brasilia in 1960 (or Australia did when it assigned the role of capital to the smaller, inland city of Canberra in 1908, away from the large power houses of Sydney and Melbourne) could serve as a model.

We know as a fact that the population of the US is fleeing the North East to other parts of the country, and the time has come to enshrine that reality by moving the President's House to the center of the mainland; such entity would easily be the second (and largest) territory making up the federal district. Finally, the Supreme Court needs to be moved to the Western lands, preferably to Santa Fe, New Mexico, to make our Supreme Court Justices aware of the impact that Mexican culture has had on the growth of this great country. The current Supreme Court building in the capital could be turned into a Presidential Museum that would prevent future Presidents from creating monuments to themselves in the form of presidential libraries.

No one takes seriously any longer the separation of powers that were incorporated by our Founding Fathers into our Constitution. By separating the District of Columbia into three sections, we enable the concept of "separation of powers" to cease being a meaningless string of words and instead we make it palpable and visible, for Americans themselves and the world to see. Modern technologies allow for instant communications between all branches of government, and the bureaucracy can be restrained by law from flying away to other parts of the district to conduct official business. That way, all bureaucratic consultations and discussions can be recorded for future posterity, thereby achieving full transparency in government. The new democratic America will offer easier access to truly divided government.

We believe that, if we really want to bring back checks and balances, members of our governing elite must be separated through physical distance. The removal of capitals from their historical locations has been done in the past both in the United States and many other countries.

As a reminder of how to expand the intuition of the Founding Fathers regarding institutions that enshrine the "essential and inherent rights" of people (in the expression of John Adams, referring to natural rights), we propose an amendment on national elections' ballot box. It would be called the Early Vote and Ballot Lockdown Amendment. While a voter registration will be required (a voter card could be obtained at Federal locations such as post offices), all computation of ballots will only happen after Hawaii has cast its ballots by 8:00 p.m. local time. It is obvious that political strategies are used to call the outcome of a presidential election early, and stop any trend that will undo the power elites on the East Coast. Because the polls close three hours earlier on the East Coast than on the West Coast, and five hours earlier than in Hawaii, the Western states do not have a voice of comparable value. That needs to be changed.

All these amendments—singly and in the aggregate—and also the potential for other meaningful ones, will be a reminder to those on the left and on the right that complaining about the imperial Presidency is cheap: There is a need to take actions, and not simply utter words, to promote effective change in the course of this great nation.

NOTES

1. Most Americans have no clear idea of the large number of race riots that have occurred in this country. While it is easy to obtain a list of all those riots in the Internet, for the 20th century, the readers may want to consult Walter C. Rucker and James N. Upton, editors, *Encyclopedia of American Race Riots*, two volumes (Westport, CT: Greenwood Press, 2006).

2. If the reader had to consult this note, he or she most likely did not know the answer. The authors found that, years ago, college students could not answer the question, but more recently they rush to their phones and get the answer right away: Charles Curtis, Senate Majority Leader and then Vice President under President Herbert Hoover (1929-1933). The authors find it amazing that most Republicans (including Ann Coulter) are not even aware of (or fail to recall) this significant historical figure. It is like asking college students who was the first black American to win the Nobel Peace Prize; they have no clue, responding incorrectly that it was Dr. Martin Luther King. The answer is Ralph Bunche, who won it in 1950.

Chapter Fourteen

The Obstacles That We Still Face

The concept of the "sovereign" has appeared in previous chapters, and we now want to spell out its meaning in some details. The concept is normally defined as the supreme authority within a territory. This means, of course, that the sovereign may consist of a political party, a dictator, a junta, a king, the members of a theocracy or even "the people," when these rule through a constitution. Does it make a difference who happens to be the supreme authority?

The answer is not entirely clear. One person or even one party cannot rule effectively over a large group of people that makes up a nation in the modern sense of the word. The person or the party would require many supporters to be able to enforce its will. Therefore, one is bound to see some individuals who benefit from the rule of the sovereign but also encounter others whose rights are trampled and curtailed. Even when "We the People" ruled via a constitution, such as was the case in the early history of the United States, the American government allowed for slavery and the human rights of slaves were violated and trampled by many citizens.

The point we make is twofold: no form of government will necessarily guarantee human rights to all the people, but some governments will come closer to providing some guarantees to many people. A magnanimous king may, if properly motivated, establish a government that conceivably respects universal rights to life, liberty and property (including self-ownership). Examples are few and far between, but the model of Cyrus the Great (especially as revealed in *Cyropaedia*, a biography of Cyrus the Great written by Xenophon, a Greek historian) was well known to scholars and their students in antiquity down to Machiavelli and others in modern times. This testimony shows a ruler supposedly capable of winning the trust of his subjects.

We are bound to observe many differences in how sovereigns control their territories. Yet, when one goes back in time, to the bands and tribes and kingdoms that gave rise to the modern states, one observes how coercion or defeat in war played a dominant role in the establishment of all governance structures. Modern states resulted from the amalgamation of various kingdoms and similar entities, and the elements of coercion and conquest were paramount. The same was true for empires, whether in the classical periods of Cyrus's Persian empire, Rome and Byzantium or in their modern incarnations of China and the Soviet Union.

Colonies and their modern descendants are no exceptions; the Spanish and the English empires destroyed existing states, and while colonists could call upon the history of the colonial powers to develop their own institutions, coercion and conquest continued to be exercised by modern states against native populations, imported African slaves and ethnic or religious minorities within their borders. To claim otherwise is simply to be ignorant of history.

One does not need to be judgmental; but one has to be realistic. There is no doubt that the founding fathers of some modern states had high moral principles when they were trying to forge new nations, but at the same time they could not ignore the historical circumstances in which they found themselves. The founders of our own country had great respect for property, for example, which forced them to acquiesce in the institution of slavery; but we must recognize that the rebels who fought the war of American independence did not respect the property of those who supported the British.

History is a tragic story, and the sovereign is part and parcel of that tragedy; for once someone, or some group of people, or some successful movement gains the power of coercion— which is the defining characteristic of a supreme authority within a territory—one is bound to observe laws that favor one group over another, restrictions on the choices of some individuals, and the abuse of government power. Founders might discuss what the ideal governance structure might look like, but no matter how much they try, in the end, partisanships arise and the citizens end up confronting the problem of which partisans to support. States are forged in history and in particular circumstances, no matter which ideals motivate the founders.

It is important to accept this realistic notion of the origin of all states, while at the same time trying to improve the governing structures which we all currently face. This notion is commonsensical enough, yet it also aligns with recommendations made by Immanuel Kant. Everyone (including us) is caught up in his and her particular historical circumstances, yet we accept the goal of improving the moral fabric of society. This requires from us total respect for the choices that other people make, even when these choices disagree with those that we make. It requires above all else the defense of the right to make choices, and the awareness that all choices are made in an uncertain environment. While we should be driven in our behavior by the moral duties that we set for ourselves, we must recognize that political ideologies and personal interests influence even our behavior. Recognizing our own moral failures facilitate our being charitable to the moral failures of others.

To illustrate the above perspective, let us briefly turn once again to the issue of slavery. Let us think of people in America in the 1830s and 1840s. Most of them did not participate in the decisions that gave the new country the rule of law—first the Articles of Confederation and later the Constitution of the United States. They were born in America, and they generally accepted the institutions that they encountered—whether born free or slave. Since it is difficult to imagine alternatives to the status quo, most people took slavery for granted. When some individuals came up with ideas that opposed the status quo, suddenly the vast majority of the population found themselves in the unpleasant position of taking sides and making choices. For the slaves, the choice was to remain in shackles or to flee north; for the non-slave the choice was to keep supporting the sovereign, which enforced slavery, or to try to change the behavior of the sovereign in order to defend the right to freedom of all human beings.

While the rest of the story is history, this history could have been written in a very different way. Since slavery was written into the Constitution, it was incumbent upon the citizens to respect the founding document of the nation and try to purchase the freedom of the slaves. While some could argue that the 1830s and 1840s generations had not signed on to the Constitution, the citizens had the option of leaving the country—and by failing to do so they were implicit signatories to the founding document. The slaves were not counted as citizens and for them open rebellion or escape was mandatory—if they had understood that no one had the right to curtail their freedom. Regrettably, everyone (including the slaves) was born into the mores of the status quo.

People think that they belong to one or another nationality by birth, as if this right was conferred by a Divine pronouncement. We have only one right by birth: the right to our freedom, which is conferred upon us by our humanity. This freedom is based upon our ability to make choices after we use our reasoning powers to decide which is best for us. Logic requires that we all have freedom, for otherwise logic itself would be inconsistent.

All Americans today have the right to citizenship by birth, but that right is conferred by a document that happens to be the Constitution, as amended after the Civil War. But since we have an intrinsic freedom to reject even that document, when we accept to live in America, we must give the Constitution our hearts and souls. We all *choose* to be Americans. While the slaves (noncitizens then) had the right to rebel or flee, the citizens had the duty to work within the Constitution to grant the slaves their freedom—for that was part of their moral duty. The Civil War was not the solution of the problem: it was the purchase of the slaves—because citizens had the moral obligation to avoid bloodshed (which also infringed upon the humanity of others).

What conclusions must we draw? People have the natural inclination to accept the status quo—which may or may not accord with our moral views, once they are closely examined. The sovereign, by definition, is the enforcer of the laws, which are unlikely to defend all of our freedoms. To make the Constitution meaningful, it should be subjected to periodic evaluations by the people, to make them aware of the documents that bind them together—and to force them to recognize the limitations that are ingrained in all such documents, for they are written by partisans and not by gods.

The truly relevant question is this: How should our constitutions change over time? Constitutions, of course, define our rights to property. Most Native Americans were not originally granted rights to the lands that they occupied—or when they were granted those rights by the legal system, they were arbitrarily revoked, leading to tremendous tragedy and suffering. Slaves were not even granted self-ownership, and again they encountered tragedy and suffering. Religious minorities (the Mormons and the Jews) had either to change their beliefs or lifestyles to be full members of the community, or accept widespread discrimination. If we want constitutions that defend our personal freedoms, we must defend above all else the right to private property.

We do not yet have full rights to private property. These rights include the right to buy and sell commodities in domestic and international markets, via voluntary transactions. The state should not intervene in what anyone buys or sells, or influence the prices that competitive markets establish. Most countries of the world prevent free trade, especially in the areas of the arts and information. Well-known universities in the developed world are required to obtain special permits to establish themselves abroad, and the film and television industries face national restrictions throughout the world. Land is not available for sale to foreigners in most countries of the world, and foreign business enterprises face special restrictions to establish themselves in both rich and poor countries.

If we had true freedom to engage in trade, in America and elsewhere, everyone would be able to hold domestic accounts in foreign currencies, and the sovereigns would be unable to control the money supply in any one country of the world. Legal tender would be determined by the voluntary choices of people, and not by the sovereigns ruling those people. Sovereigns' control over domestic money supplies means control over interest rates, when these should rather reflect voluntary transactions worldwide.

Sovereigns have the power to tax, to regulate, to borrow abroad and to print money. While the first two powers are compatible with our freedoms, when exercised wisely, the power to borrow abroad and to print money gives all sovereigns the ability to impose their partisan interests upon the rest of the population. This is especially true when it comes to wars, which should be approved, at the very least, by a referendum of the population. Both the Bush and the Obama administrations have allowed China to maintain non-market clearing prices for the goods and services that China trades in international markets. While this has allowed the American consumers to buy cheap goods abroad, it has also allowed China to accumulate foreign reserves which are then borrowed by the US government—with the purpose of using them to pay for the wars that American citizens are unwilling to pay for! Rivalries and cooperation among sovereigns of the world allow for tragic wars that violate the intrinsic human rights of those impacted by war.

While this chapter presents a pessimistic view of the prospects that we face when we attempt to change our institutions, it is necessary to get to know the obstacles that we face. All governments originate as the result of war and coercion, including our own (particularly with regards to the native populations and the black slaves). We are privileged to have a Constitution that guarantees some of our rights. Yet even that Constitution allows the government to borrow money from abroad, to create domestic currency out of thin air, to form international alliances that do not serve the interests of the citizens, to revoke rights that are not entrenched in the Constitution, to restrict our rights to engage in free trade and, most important, to force us to use the domestic currency as legal tender. While it is true that we need to change our moral values if we are to create new institutional structures (as we have argued in other chapters) we must also recognize the political obstacles that we face as we try to augment our freedoms.

Chapter Fifteen

The Road to Wealth Creation in a Society with Meaningful Lives

We have described, in previous chapters, how to rebuild our moral foundations, how to change our institutions to gain greater independence, and how to achieve individual self-actualization, while providing assistance to those in need. We have been both general and specific in our analyses, going to the extreme, in Chapter 13, of suggesting specific constitutional amendments that would help us achieve our goals. We have asserted on various occasions that our goal is not to make people happy, but rather to make sure that they have meaningful lives. But the readers may wonder if the road that we have traced for them would also make us wealthier. This is a relevant question that we now address. Is it the case, for example, that limiting the size of government might lead to lower rates of economic growth? This is a perfectly legitimate question that needs a balanced and responsible answer.

It should be obvious to the readers that governments take on activities that could easily be done by private enterprise, such as the provision of schools, healthcare, and a large number of insurance-related activities. This does not mean that the government has no role to play in these activities; it means that their *provision* is best achieved in the private sector. For instance, it is in the best interest of the nation to provide schooling to the younger generation, but that does not mean that the schooling has to be done in public schools, but rather that all children should have access to the necessary resources to go to the private schools that best serve their interests. Hence the government can guarantee (and use the power of taxation to obtain the necessary funds) children's access to schools that best serve their needs. In principle, at least, the private sector can provide the schooling, healthcare and other insurance-related activities that the government provides—and most likely, provide them more efficiently.

We state "more efficiently" because the costs of these activities then become transparent, and because the demand for the goods or services is not determined via the political process, which requires legislative actions and compromises, as we saw in Chapter 9. Public schools are paid for from a variety of sources. The federal government and the states subsidize educational costs, expenditures which are not visible in local taxes. School budgets at the municipal level, too, fail to include such items as insurance and a variety of maintenance costs, thereby hiding the true costs of the services provided when the school budgets are presented to local populations. Private schools, in contrast, need to consider all of the costs involved when they determine their budgets, and then charge the appropriate tuition.

There is no doubt, however, that some economic projects are so large that they cannot be undertaken by the private sector, especially when it comes to their financing. Such is the case for some infrastructure projects, where the payoff is widespread and possibly unknown. However, even if the costs and benefits were easy to determine, it would make economic sense to provide them at a loss, since the major costs of these projects are the fixed costs; yet efficiency requires that consumers be charged the costs of running the projects once they are completed—which would not be enough to pay for the fixed costs. (The reader can imagine a huge subway system that, once built, is relatively cheap to run.) No private enterprise would be willing to put together a large project where the fixed costs could not be recovered; in those cases, the project must be undertaken by the government or, at the very least, financed with the assistance of government subsidies.

The point of the above, which can easily involve national defense, space programs, and what economists call "public goods" (a technical term, not simply goods provided by the government), clearly justifies the government's involvement in the economy, under restricted conditions.[1] Regrettably, governments often ignore these restricted conditions and engage in activities which are clearly destructive of wealth rather than wealth-creating. Readers must have surely heard of bridges that lead to nowhere! Or subsidized companies (Solyndra comes to mind) that are unable to sell their products under competitive conditions.

Let us then take a closer look at wealth-destructive events or activities, even when the government is not responsible for most of them. This approach will allow us to understand how wealth creation can be achieved.

Wealth refers to some asset that can potentially generate future income streams—in other words, some asset that can be put to productive use. So, wealth is not created when it is stolen, for that is simply a deceptive means of acquiring useful assets; existing wealth is simply transferred. Wealth is not created when someone discovers some productive asset by chance—in that case the asset just happens to be useful; wealth is discovered but not created. Wealth is not created when the government imposes restrictions on the *search* for assets, or prevents existing assets from being used *productively*. Wealth is destroyed by many factors: intentional or unintentional fires, by hurricanes, tsunamis, earthquakes, wars, and natural catastrophes of every type. Wealth is misused when the owner of the asset fails to use it efficiently. Surprisingly, wealth can also be destroyed by innovations—and there lies the rub!

But how is wealth created? We are accustomed to imagine that the main source of wealth creation is through savings and investments—in other words, through the accumulation of capital. Strictly speaking, that generates an insignificant amount of wealth creation. The reason is best illustrated with a historical example: no matter how much our ancestors saved and invested, if they kept the same technologies, they would have remained poor. When technological change becomes part of the new capital assets, then we have wealth creation—therefore, innovations are the main sources of wealth creation (but also of wealth destruction, as we shall see). Competitive markets help immensely in the allocation of the new assets.

Wealth is generated in many other ways. The agglomeration of people serves to increase the size of the market and allows for greater specialization. The technologies might not even be too different from the technologies already known; what large markets allow is for the use of capital goods that incorporate more specialized but known technologies. The existing technologies can change, too, because of economies of scale and the development of more efficient market signals.

Markets increase wealth for another reason: specialization in trade. Since different people have different tastes, and the costs of production vary across regions due to natural and manmade cost differentials, markets provide us with a better allocation of resources. When trade is voluntary, many gains result from trade. Trading activities, however, can also result in wealth destruction—at least for some participants, to be discussed below.

Peace and security also brings wealth creation. A counterexample serves to illustrate the idea. The September 11, 2001 attacks reduced peace and security. Since everyone felt threatened by the terrorist attacks, policies were enacted to return to the normal peace and security levels— thereby devoting old resources to these new activities. The use of these resources made everyone else poorer, for the resources had been producing other goods and services that provided the consumers greater satisfaction. Regrettably, the recent threats and actions of Islamic radicals in Europe and elsewhere are destructive of wealth, for similar reasons.

Some economists argue that people are truly the only source of wealth creation, for it is people who discover new technologies, new institutional arrangements, new potential assets, and are ultimately responsible to put these assets to work. Hence, human capital is extremely important as our ultimate resource, both in terms of the training that humans acquire and the technologies that they create. Regrettably, humans also have natural tendencies to dominate, to prevent others from acquiring that which enhances their human capital, to create price distortions in markets, and most importantly to engage in wars against one another. Humans, when not restrained by moral values, can be as destructive as they can be creative.

We have argued that humans find themselves conflicted: on the one hand they have the natural inclinations that all animals possess, yet on the other hand their reasoning powers insist on the quest for rules of behavior that force them to engage in self-reflection, and gnaw them to consider the impact of their behavior on others. Moral behavior has the potential of enhancing wealth creation.

Surprisingly, while the introduction of new technologies gives rise to wealth creation, it also leads to the destruction of previously existing wealth. Is this an indication that personal freedoms can give rise to the destruction of property rights? The answer is obviously no. The reason is simple. People acquire property, meaning in most cases the right to use both physical and abstract assets, with the intention of using those assets productively—in other words, converting the assets into generators of income streams or what we know as wealth. Yet no one can guarantee the success of this endeavor because it is uncertain, rather than risky (in other words, insurance on innovation is impossible!) Hence people retain their private property rights, even though their assets may become worthless. Technological change can destroy wealth, but not property rights.

This process can be extremely painful, not just within a country but also across countries. The introduction of the automobile destroyed the wealth of producers of horse-drawn carriages. The construction of roads reduced the profitability of trains. Airplanes changed the way people moved from one country to another. The computer destroyed secretarial services. Petroleum destroyed the importance of whale oil. And all this occurred because people were free to make choices and use their reasoning powers to generate new options in both production and consumption.

These changes are also reflected in the history of international trade. Some countries faced competition from products that they had no way of predicting would come into the market. Hence products that at one time sold well across international markets, such as hand-made clothing, shoes and hats, were suddenly replaced with machine-made products that lasted longer, were generally far more attractive and, most importantly, could be produced far cheaper.

The real problem with technological change is that no one, absolutely no one, has been able to predict its course accurately. If such predictions were possible, then insurance would be possible, as previously stated. Whereas individuals in particular regions can insure themselves against hurricanes and some (but not all) natural disasters, they cannot insure themselves against market forces—and that is what makes competitive markets frightful and government interventions palatable.

Hence governments have found a way of making themselves useful—pretending that they can insure people against events that are uninsurable—and often enough paying for that insurance by borrowing from abroad.[2] Wars are also uninsurable events, and oftentimes governments promote them. Hitler achieved popularity with his aggressive policies. Yet, if the people of Germany had known the consequences of the Hitler regime, everyone would have bought insurance against the unforeseen destruction of the war—but that type of insurance was impossible. A supposedly serious politician in America said: "you never want a serious crisis to go to waste;" and a Machiavellian ruler could add: and we can create the crisis ourselves! For those of us who have lived in revolutionary times, it is clear that those who engage in revolution create crises. Shooting mass protesters, by those who *organize the protest marches* against the government, is nothing new; yet former organizers who later have a change of heart describe such actions.[3]

In conclusion, then, stability within a nation is conducive to wealth creation—which originates mainly through technological change. Wealth creation requires an educated labor force, entrepreneurs willing to gamble their future, large markets, the agglomeration of people to take advantage of economies of scale, and competitive markets that help guide the allocation of resources. But technical change also brings forth wealth destruction, as old methods of production are discarded and various human skills become obsolete.

NOTES

1. The literature on public goods is enormous. The reader may search the term in David R. Henderson, ed. *The Concise Encyclopedia of Economics,* http://www.econlib.org/library/CEE.html, to obtain a large number of dependable books and articles on the subject.

2. The difference between risk and uncertainty (when events are insurable and uninsurable, respectively) is widely understood in economics and statistics. Regrettably, this distinction has yet to make a dent in political circles, mainly because of its technical nature. However, there is now an excellent, yet popular book, that covers the distinction to perfection; see Gerd Gigerenzer, *Risk Savvy; How to Make Good Decisions* (New York: Viking, 2014). The authors highly recommend the many works of the author, who is the Director of the Max Planck Institute for Human Development in Berlin, Germany.

3. See Ramon L. Bonachea and Marta San Martin, *The Cuban Insurrection, 1952-1959* (New Brunswick, NJ: Transaction Publishers, 1974). This book will give the reader an idea of how a revolution is conducted.

Chapter Sixteen

Imperialism as a Threat to American Governance

The question about the United States' global dominance is whether its pre-eminence and influence on the world stage is one more case of imperial power, reaching its zenith in the aftermath of World War II and subsequently becoming problematic and shrinking.[1] Is it the fate of the United States to repeat the imperialism of the European powers and exploit distant lands and weaker peoples by means of monopolistic commercialism (combined with militarism)? Global American interventionism is a well established trait of the 20th century, which stands as a testament to the United States success in prevailing in two World Wars and in terminating the Cold War with the Soviet empire. And yet, as the Chinese empire stands resurgent and new economic powerhouses emerge in Asia and possibly South America, a question remains: How will the world be dependent on the policy of free trade, if the Americans are unable to affirm their commitment to it? Has Manifest Destiny finally misfired in the face of its heirs?

Obviously, the United States didn't acquire sovereignty over a significant landmass (and create its considerable internal markets) overnight. Since the time of the founding of the Republic, various steps would be taken, stretching over the better part of the 19th century: it started with the Louisiana purchase, continued with the Western expansion, and then the incorporation of Texas at the end of the Mexican War. Finally, the retreat of Spain from her empire (in Cuba and the Philippines) led to a monopoly of American hemispheric power with the notion that lands in the Americas or nearby (Hawaii and Alaska—Puerto Rico and other islands) would, and should, fall under its Federal laws or under its direct influence.

American supremacy—or Manifest Destiny—also necessitated a significant population increase (enabled by the various Homestead Acts from 1850 to 1916) and a spectacular growth of industrial power. Manifest Destiny—the idea that settling a continent through the power of American freedom was inevitable—took many steps, each combining considerable foresight and the will to maintain political power over the warring commercial interests: this had required the soft power of individual energies (the American Dream on tap at the feet of the Statue of Liberty) and the vision of federal policies (Alexander Hamilton as their architect) helping domestic commerce and ensuring its protection from foreign threats.

As scholars and as individuals, we must guard from the tendency to believe that events necessarily shape our thinking. Still, geography and the glue of culture played decisive roles in opening the American continent to the experiment of a new order (*Novus ordo seclorum*). Progress could have evolved differently, along different lines, especially concerning the aftermath of slavery, the failure of Reconstruction and the scourge of segregation—yet the promise of America in delivering goods and freedom had to combine the formal power of internal constitutionalism and the informal power of the American Dream firing up so many lives.[2] As wealth grew and life opportunities developed, the complementarity of the formal American empire and the informal power of wealth and opportunity may have started to fray—especially after the Vietnam War.

But we need to be reminded of some historical truths. The quandary of imperial tyranny, which locks power and control to benefit an oligarchy, was well-known to Locke, Montesquieu, Burke, the U.S. Founding Fathers, Cobden, Bastiat,[3] and Gladstone. The entire group of English and American Whig (anti-Tory)[4] revolutionaries devised a series of institutional and cultural mechanisms for restricting the oligarchic tendencies and opening up the process of soft power of wealth creation. Yet, have these institutional mechanisms and their cultural harmony with "progress" been overrun by the realities of a government on steroids, the progressives' idea that there is nothing that the government elite cannot tackle, take to task, and control for the benefit of . . . "We the People"?

Single absolute power and control over the lives of all who come into contact with its army and its laws—such is traditional imperialism. An empire is constituted at home when the threat of exerting political domination and unleashing violence against (former) restraints is made good.

In Western history this happened when Caesar crossed the Rubicon and his advancing armies told all that they had seized the day and the republic was at an end. There was a sizable increase in the power and control heaped on the body politic in times of "peace." In the case of ancient Rome there were a good number of men willing to assist Brutus in dispatching the tyrant to the underworld, but Caesar had accustomed the masses to largesse—the famed bread and circus—and it was they who forced the deification of the tyrant by the Senate. Subsequently, Western civilization has been plagued by the reverential Caesar derivatives/titles of Kaiser or Czar among its phoenix-like lines of empires, the adulation of serial killers of many stripes, from Alexander of Macedon to Napoleon and Stalin (all of whom died in their beds, not at the hand of a Brutus).

The logic of empire and controlled dependencies, also, has had a long line of apologists in the intellectual arsenal of Western civilization. It is hard not to agree with the American constitutionalists that there is something amiss in our tradition if the "quarrel between the ancients and the moderns"[5] concludes with the top academic recognition being bestowed upon empire builders/destroyers such as Alexander, Caesar, Napoleon, Lenin and Stalin.

It is also true that the intellectual arsenal against free trade as the key to commerce and wealth creation harkens back to Plato's *Republic* and under various guises extends to us through the modern theories of Machiavelli, Rousseau, Hegel, Marx and Lenin—all of who advocated the absolute power of the state wielded by a state creator for the people, that must be guarded against ignorant and unwieldy internal opponents.

The American Founding Fathers, in contrast, declared that the birth of the American Republic—a nation bringing all sovereign colonies into a shared, organized destiny—was tantamount to a new experiment in political organization. The Founders enabled a new political body to take its place among the powers of the earth; yet they were keenly aware that an empire of ideas would be needed to prevent the slide of the people towards an imperial model of dependency. Jefferson anticipated that Liberty would periodically need a refresher course in what it denotes and connotes—with the corollary of staying clear of governmental intrusion.

"Life, Liberty and Property" are the key terms articulated by the proponents of the natural rights against the ownership of the public realm by the entitled elites. These terms emerged in the English Whigs and they continued their insistent claims in the various colonial charters, state constitutions, even prior to the Federal Constitution. A constitution without these terms as their premises would be empty and without substance.

It is well known that the phrase "pursuit of happiness" was introduced in lieu of property. When students of history look at the extraordinary looting and plundering that initiated the mass totalitarian movements in Europe and the world, it is hard for them to deny that without property, private and public happiness are impossible. These empires of controlled dependencies got under way when a central power acquired and never let go of the means to deny individuals their natural rights, and when elites took over previous institutional arrangements—enabling them to control people by edicts, propaganda, and repression of information and debate.

All men know that wealth creation is the purpose of economic life. The attraction of a wealth to be plundered is what attracted Alexander to the riches of Asia. With the end of the pillage, the Greeks brought back stories of heroism rivalling Homer's epic poems. The fascination of wealth on a large scale is what opened the career of the world's conquerors, and their determination to reach immortal glory at whatever cost. The attraction of plunder is what drove Caesar to Gaul and soon enough he shared his bounties with the people (along with the propaganda he penned), but his generosity to the Romans cost the lives of a whopping twenty percent of the Gallic population and the amputation of all able-bodied men who had fought his legions.

Commercial nations are interested in their welfare and the continuation of business transactions rather than in the advantages of plunder. This is a cultural reason why they shun the rule of conquest. Some could argue that it might be the other way around, with geography preventing them from direct or simple expansion. Consider the Swiss, the Dutch and the old Venetians, who held their republics at arm's length from those larger entities whose cultural DNA was impregnated with the virus of empire and plunder.

John Locke, Montesquieu, Adam Smith and Kant shared in the same assessment of wealth creation as weaving a fabric of proper civilization, mild manners and preparing a path for the greater emotions and virtues of empathy and "fellow-feeling." In his recent book *America*,[6] Dinesh D'Souza makes the legitimate claim that empathy for others and the concern for impartial spectators are at the very core of capitalist entrepreneurship. Empires of plunder have come and gone, empires of wealth creation have emerged— and by logical consistency the latter must have arisen first. The Roman empire of plunder could only set itself in motion by the earlier transformation of the republic into an acquisitive machine whose legions were motivated by the lure of bounties, lands and political office—advertising this conquering program to whomever might lend assistance. Chilling among Machiavelli's writings are his descriptions of Rome "who became great by ruining her neighboring cities and by freely admitting strangers to her privileges and honors," Crescit interea Roma, Albae ruinis (All this time Rome grew on the ruins of Alba).[7]

This program was kept up or intensified until the Roman holocaust of Carthage,[8] whose commercial empire the Romans could not but destroy, but whose strategically essential industries (especially olive oil and wheat) they brought under Roman patronage.

Large scale monopolistic production and the discovery of economies of scale through pre-modern, industrial production were born together and routinely demonstrated in the feeding of the Roman metropolis. But no doubt too it was true that Roman wealth was also made to grow by the countless, uprooted individuals of the empire who saw business opportunities in Rome and the other cities of the empire, where they benefited from a large-scale marketplace of consumers and customers. Roman wealth, created in these conditions, would necessarily become both a lure and an irritant for the people not quite ready to be subjugated—the Britons, the Germanic tribes, and the pesky tribes of the lower Danube.

Scholars often comment that it was two factors—the mild manners of Christianity (untainted by absolute monarchy, and re-energized by the Puritans' ethos of civil disobedience toward absolutism) and the elevation of the sciences into the curriculum taught in the universities of the Middle Ages—that presented the most distinguishing differential characteristics between the modern era and ancient Rome. Americans enshrined these two traits—the tolerance of Christianity and the preeminence of science in education—in their institutions and, indirectly although firmly, into their Constitution. By untangling religion from the commission of civil penalty—and denying civil penalties the aura of religion—the Founding Fathers defined the limits to follow in the empire of ideas to guide the republic.

Likewise, science and right opinion—formed by looking at all theories without limitation and prejudice—formed a leading motto of the first state constitution, that of Massachusetts. This extended to the cultural DNA of America at large. It was clearly up to the states, to the communities, and to the families to decide how best to educate their children. Competition and striving for excellence were unspoken and accepted. They were made possible by (but they also greatly contributed to) these two aspects of American soft power: an egalitarianism of opportunities as well as guided assistance.[9] It is these two that are at the core of the informal, cultural empire of ideas that defines the American extension of Whig culture to the new continent. But we now ask, Is "Manifest Destiny" at an end? The answer is an educated "Maybe yes, maybe no," which we now proceed to explain.

The charge of outright imperialism attempting to rule the world and projecting American hegemony on poor countries stems from a series of facts that can be construed as repeated failures in foreign policy. Formal empire (invasions, gunboat diplomacy, and threats, as well as bribes, to independent countries) is at the core of that charge. Instead of a path to economic and political development that is regulated by the country's internal laws, American foreign policy is depicted as prone to intervene and dictate choices that American corporate interests have made clear to Washington power brokers. This tendency, it is pointed out, originates in the monopoly of power projected on the Americas—let us recall that the Monroe Doctrine was up-ended by the Roosevelt Corollary and his Big Stick Diplomacy. It appears that the tactical advantages of particular economic interests translated into hot spots of muscular American foreign meddling. The evidence lies in the fact that, starting with the construction of the Panama Canal and the subservience of Cuba to the U.S., Central American countries could not define their own political and economic paths, which were essentially dictated to by Washington.

But formal empire is not the only explanation, since the soft power of American commerce and products, the allure of American innovations as well as humanitarianism were part of the package given to the Central American and Caribbean nations. Immigration from those countries to the United States was a feature not less constant than the immigration from traditional European sources.[10] Subsequently, the outcome of the Second World War devolved control of the Pacific to the United States. This was made possible by the defeat of Japan and its successful rebuilding, the marginalization of Communist China, and the containment of communism in Korea.

From the Roosevelt Corollary to global hegemony, the path could only be chartered after a decisive and profound American intervention had taken place in Western Europe—by defeating Nazi Germany and rebuilding the war-torn countries by means of the Marshall Plan. But here again, we see not so much a direct influence of militarism as a combination of the tools of formal empire with those of informal power. The rebuilding of Japan and Europe, the economic impetus given to South Korea, Nixon's policy change towards China and the welcoming of capitalistic structures after the Tiananmen Square massacre, are important facts and factors which indicate that American formal empire is not an end in itself, but comes to the assistance of an empire of commerce.

But the charge of American meddling and destructive imperialism was repeated with the Vietnam War, with destruction rained on innocent foreign individuals (civilians) by a series of executive decisions that did not have Congressional approval or the backing of the United States citizenry. The Vietnam War turned into a syndrome—one that gave credence to President Eisenhower's warning against the hidden influence of the "military industrial complex."

It is with that war that American public opinion started shifting against the merits of formal empire, as well as no longer grasping the need for an informal empire based on free trade. These changes coincided with the change from a draft to a professional army. Meanwhile, the intrusiveness of government continued with costly domestic programs that didn't work (the "War on Poverty"). The imperial executive orders and the agenda of President Johnson never reduced group inequalities nor eased racial tensions despite huge federal outlays—a legacy that will take great effort to undo.

We begin to see how the complementarity between formal and informal empire has been eroded in the three decades that have followed the Vietnam War. This complementarity was temporarily reasserted by Ronald Reagan in his economic success and, strikingly, in his role facilitating the dismantling of the Soviet empire. Various moving parts of that objective involved disabling the Soviet army in Afghanistan, giving support to Poland's democracy, and asserting the credibility of superior American defense technologies—

SDI or "Star Wars." This complementarity is clearly a thorn in the side of the critics of "Manifest Destiny" and American Exceptionalism. Linking formal (muscular) and informal (free trade) imperialism should promote the second and decrease the first. If Manifest Destiny is at an end, then American exceptionalism has to be proven to depend upon plunder, deception and governmental propaganda.

Academic—domestic and international—critics of American power must either equate the two elements we've distinguished while arguing for their complementarity, or they must trump both with another form of imperialism (one managed by the elites). The success of Reagan's presidency came from the fact that formal and informal empires could work in articulated synchronicity. These critics have to argue that a higher-level set of interests trumped the political decisions and that Communism directed from Moscow had been doomed for a long time. From their point of view, Reagan only precipitated a reorganization of the hidden powers-that-be. Whatever the corporate flavor, the conspiracy theories abound in that matter. It can be the unelected Federal Reserve Bank attempting to get a more global reach for its creditor clients. Or it can also be a consortium of defense corporations pushing their wares on bigger markets. It is clear these entities function under the radar, but need support from a non-transparent federal government and its elites. For the so-called "one-percenters" and the Tea Party advocates, there is a strong suspicion that in the midst of the economic and political power, there lurks a form of imperial control. Can that point, which seems to be articulated by minorities of the left and right, be made into a mainstream rational argument?

Such is what we will attempt to do in our conclusion. It is impossible to deny that the increase of government power and the intrusion of control of individuals have had devastating effects on the freedom of individuals. This is true not only domestically (see the intimidation of political opponents, which is a characteristic practice of Vladimir Putin and Lois Lerner, or even the Obama Administration) but also internationally by the programs of aid to Africa. As documented by Africans such as James Shikwati,[11] Dambisa Moyo[12] and the African Chapter of *Doctors Without Borders*, food aid not only does not solve the problems in the middle and long term, but it prevents the informal access to development and, additionally, fuels conflicts. The one trillion dollars spent on Africa's food relief since it began in the late 1940's stand as a stark reminder of a totally failed policy experiment. It was, and still is, fueled by rich government control, rich country lobbied interests, local country elite interests, and U.N. corporate welfare programs—all leading to a form of continent-wide malfeasance.

It is uncertain how long such dysfunctions would take to be undone. An informal empire of trade would greatly benefit those African countries, just the same as a regulated, but an increasingly free empire of trade was correctly deemed to benefit China, India, Brazil and other countries. But the critics

of American corporate welfare and malfeasance (whether they come internationally or domestically, whether they appear with a left-leaning or fiscal
conservative, and right-leaning, agenda) have a point. These dysfunctions are
to the detriment of the people, and they benefit elites, no longer connected
through the formal structures of nation states or even formal empires.

Since politics is always local, it behooves those with political authority
(whether they be Chinese-style mandarins or American and British-style religious humanitarians or Free Trade advocates) to seek policies of soft power
that empower individuals and maintain control through legitimacy. This soft
power speaks the language of mutual trust, of exchanges of products and
services, yet it also acknowledges that the use of a big stick must be resorted
to without hesitation in circumstances of self-defense. Critiquing the United
States for past or current meddling in the world is acceptable if solutions are
presented for empowering legitimate groups and individuals who have been
oppressed and repressed. Only informal empires of trade can argue in front of
their publics that innovation and public access to resources will increase
individual and their societies' wellbeing—and what real costs are incurred
when imperial-style governments and agencies collude and attempt to rule
secretively.

NOTES

1. Niall Ferguson, *Colossus: The Rise and Fall of the American Empire* (New York:
Penguin Books, 2004). See also his *Empire: The Rise and Demise of the British World Order
and the Lessons for Global Power* (New York: Basic Books, 2004).

2. The contrast between formal and informal empires was developed in the important
article by John Gallagher and Ronald Robinson, "The Imperialism of Free Trade," *The Economic History Review* 6, no. 1 (August 1953): 1–15.

3. See George Charles Roche III, "Frédéric Bastiat: A Man Alone," last modified October
20, 2009, accessed October. 24, 2015, https://mises.org/library/fr%C3%A9d%C3%A9ric-bas-
tiat-man-alone.

4. See Daniel Hannan, *Inventing Freedom: How the English-Speaking Peoples Made the
Modern World* (New York: HarperCollins, 2013).

5. The so-called quarrel between the ancients and the moderns plays a major role in the
unfolding of Western political philosophy and metaphysics from Machiavelli and Hobbes to
Rousseau, Hegel, Nietzsche and Heidegger. See Stanley Rosen, *The Ancients and the Moderns;
Rethinking Modernity* (New Haven, CT: Yale University Press, 1989).

6. Dinesh D'Souza, *America: Imagine A World Without Her* (Washington, DC: Regnery
Publishing, 2014).

7. See Book II, Chapter III of Niccolo Machiavelli's *The Discourses* (London: Penguin
Classics, 1998).

8. See Richard Miles, *Carthage Must Be Destroyed: The Rise and Fall of an Ancient
Civilization* (New York: Viking Press, 2012).

9. This aspect of America's soft power is evidenced in the effort to combine an enlightened
"self-focus" with an "other-focus" in ethics by traditional American or Anglo-American ethi-
cists. They start with the self-focus of egoism and show it can be made compatible with the
other-focus of generosity and altruism. The tradition goes back to David Hume and Adam
Smith, and it was continued by Josiah Royce, Bernard Williams, Harry Browne and James
Rachels.

10. Many Cuban migrants came to the United States prior to 1900 as a result of the various wars in Cuba; there were three wars of independence against Spain, all of them sending refugees to Tampa, Key West, New York City and elsewhere. This theme is explored in Louis A. Perez Jr. *On Becoming Cuban: Identity, Nationality and Culture* (Chapel Hill: University of North Carolina Press, 1999). Similarly, waves of Mexican migrants came to America as a result of the 1910-20 Mexican Revolution and the Cristero War of 1926-29. These waves are detailed in Ricardo Romo's "Responses to Mexican Immigration, 1910-1930" in ed. Michael R. Ornelas, *Beyond 1848; Readings in the Modern Chicano Historical Experience* (Dubuque, IA: Kendall Hunt Publishing, 1999) and Julia G. Young, *Mexican Exodus: Emigrants, Exiles and Refugees of the Cristero War* (New York: Oxford University Press, 2015).

11. James Shikwati, "For God's Sake, Please Stop the Aid!" Spiegel Interview with African Economics Expert, http://www.spiegel.de/international/spiegel/spiegel-interview-with-african-economics-expert-for-god-s-sake-please-stop-the-aid-a-363663.html

12. Dambisa Moyo, "Dead Aid: Why Aid Is Not Working and How There Is a Better Way for Africa" (New York: Farrar, Straus and Giroux, 2009).

Chapter Seventeen

From Ancients to Moderns

Balancing Individual Rights and Duties to Others

How should we combine individualism and altruism at the core of an ethics of responsibility? How can individual motivation of self-interest and concern for one's own welfare be not only compatible with, but a requirement for, an ethics of caring that gives one's best to others? We will answer these questions within a historical context.

We plan to show that enlightened altruism is attentive altruism, for which the individual is the building block and the indispensable chain link making up complex societies. Enlightened altruists conceive a broad span of life choices for individualists, who should be neither narrowly programmed to accomplish one task only, nor ensconced in a selfish ego unconcerned for anything happening in the wider world. On the contrary, enlightened altruists will raise the bar on other altruists to make it compelling for all to take a strong view on reciprocity.

From this broad perspective, individualists will be urged to rise to broader horizons and learn the intrinsic worth of the Golden Rule and reciprocal altruism. They, and all of us for that matter, can reach such conclusions after considering some essential teachers from Athens, Rome, the Christian era and early modern times, especially Adam Smith and Immanuel Kant.

We grant to the dedicated altruists that individualists can sometimes be selfish, grabbing, and lying about their ulterior motives. We also grant to the dedicated individualists that self-professed altruists would sometimes or even often be hypocrites, and unwilling to take a hard look at how their philosophies and preferences fare in the real world. It is fair criticism that stealing from Paul in order to give to Peter (while Mary is harping at Paul for not doing enough) shouldn't be counted as altruism and generosity. Such was the argument made in the 19th century by William G. Sumner in *The Forgotten Man*,[1] who in this case turns out to be Paul, the guy who is sent the bill and given the guilty conscience.

After exploring the main features of dispossession (plunder in war and the consequences of insolvency), we will assess the requirements of distributive justice (and a form of prescriptive ethics) in the desirable life plans for the reciprocal altruists (who advocate giving) and for individualists whose favorable life outcomes and universal values really address many beyond them and their kin.

Humans are potentially daring and curious—but also potentially lazy as well as uncaring and ignorant. From the ethical lessons we hear in tales of Homer to those of Athens' Golden Age and beyond in the ancient world, we see value being put on the intricacies of sharing the common world. There are the brave and the knave, the young challenging the older, the old confounding the young. All are identifying flaws in characters, pointing out drawbacks in solutions, tragedies in personal or collective life, and fallacies in reasoning.

In the climate of investigation and challenge made possible by competing states where individuals make all the difference, democratic individuals will not give their time, money and services to cities and peers without understanding the purpose, and the ramifications, of their contributions. They insist that self-reliance and individual discipline are essential conditions of freedom and a "life worth living." The Greek Sophist's motto "Man is the measure of all things—seen and unseen" could be viewed not only as the seal of Greek know-how or philosophic wisdom (the great achievements of Marathon) but also as a call to citywide empowerment.

The citizens of Athens' Golden Age had that objective in mind: All great things were to be measured by the active participation of equals in public life. Pericles, their most famous statesman, contrasted the active Athenian members of the city with those men who just went along and never cared to shape opinion on what was good or not good, by branding them "useless." Not being wealthy is not debility, he said in his famous *Funeral Oration* (transmitted to us by Thucydides in Book 2 of *The Story of the Peloponnesian War*),[2] for it is one thing to confess poverty, but an entirely different thing "not to try to change it." Pericles stressed that in their system the same men took care of both their own and the public affairs.

The man who meddles in various things is "not useless," what makes him useless would be his blindly accepting somebody else's views and never challenging any part of them. By contrast, in Athens, Pericles said, "we weigh what we undertake and consider those things in advance in our minds, not viewing debates as hindering action—because hindrance to action comes from not having had the prior debate. For also in this we excel others, daring to undertake as much as any and yet examining what we undertake; whereas with other men it is ignorance that makes them dare, and consideration of consequences weaklings." The two characteristics of the classical Greek world were in display: friendship and challenge, in combination, made individuals more free and capable of overcoming their own weaknesses.

Men will pick up the calls for friendly emulation and respond to questions others will pose, sometimes naggingly, to overcome an individual's deficiencies. They will also learn from the blind spots that they see in others and ponder whether there might not be the same flaws, a hubris in themselves as well—which, unchecked, could lead to catastrophe.

Socrates is the other formidable Athenian who argued that man's thoughtful thinking detects the measure of all things—but that measure is hidden in the realities themselves and is itself an integral part of the organized world, or the cosmos. Socrates didn't think that individualism without the check of a "Know Thyself" examination would be conducive to a "life worth living." The most potent activity—that of thinking—necessarily involved a dialogue of the soul with itself about the world—away from the ignorance of the many and the arrogance of the few. The Socratic investigation checked hubris and was a spur to virtue or excellence.

The ethics of responsibility that Socrates promoted (as evidenced in Xenophon's *Memorabilia*, a much more accurate transmission of the real Socrates than Plato's creative stagings) involved Socrates questioning real individuals and their consideration of general questions, with a range of specific answers. The gamut of an individual's aptitudes and thinking would always be matched against the best expectations and exhortations that the city has for its citizens.

Such expectations and exhortations would be that the person be considerate, not grabbing, self-controlled yet tenacious, eager for the right recognition but also dismissive of disparagement from people swayed by the controlling demagogues. The enlightened individualist inspired by Socrates would need to combine both the silent desire of not being put upon, and the strenuous altruism of sharing the common good of freedom—being a "midwife" of the best ideas among one's contemporaries and exposing the contradictions of bad arguments.

Slightly after the Roman Republic lost its hold on the Romans (in the age of Sulla) and veered toward Empire, the Stoic and eclectic philosophies originating in Athens and imported to Rome yielded important principles for a rational ethics. These were the principles that an educated Roman would think necessary for the commonwealth. Instead of powerful individuals grabbing more control over goods, properties, and individuals than they could manage for their own sake, a cosmopolitan perspective pointed out how the physical world operated, how logical connections could or could not be made, and how in action, your focus and your intent entailed the necessity of long-term success or inescapable catastrophe.

Cicero argued that ethics properly understood—as connecting the personal and civic duties—was immediately different from self-serving expediency, and led to a pattern of reciprocal altruism. His wisdom reminds us to be mindful of what we can and cannot do, decide what we should do, and then to do it—as well as by example encourage others to do the same, such are the ways ethics supplements nature. Let "each one retain possession of that which has fallen to his lot; and if anyone appropriates to himself anything beyond that, he will be violating the laws of human society."

Cicero approved of Plato's pluralistic and anti-selfish principles that argued that we are not born for ourselves alone, but in fact for both our country and our friends—both of whom can rightfully claim a "share of our being." Yet Cicero also said that "everything that the earth produces is created for man's use; and as men, too, are born for the sake of men, they may be able mutually to help one another; in this direction we ought to follow Nature as our guide, to contribute to the general good by an interchange of acts of kindness, by giving and receiving, and thus by our skill, our industry, and our talents to cement human society more closely together, man to man" (Cicero, *On Obligations*, paragraph 20, section VII).

The foundation of justice is nature's symbiosis of species and individuals of different ages. This symbiosis extends into the moral realm of trustworthiness and good faith. At the basis of all interactions, there is a reciprocal understanding, a two-way signaling of intentions, first understood, then approved and formally accepted. It makes each act a dual commitment, worth entering into and benefiting from. Rascals and those who shrink back in silence are the target of Cicero's criticisms. "There are . . . two kinds of injustice—the one, on the part of those who inflict wrong, the other on the part of those who, when they can, do not shield from wrong those upon whom it is being inflicted. For he who, under the influence of anger or some other passion, wrongfully assaults another seems, as it were, to be laying violent hands upon a comrade; but he who does not prevent or oppose wrong, if he can, is just as guilty of wrong as if he deserted his parents or his friends or his country."

It is clear that in Cicero's account—made at the time of the inescapable foreboding of the death of the Roman Republic—more than two categories of men are needed to account for the moral wellbeing or moral decay/collapse of a society—not merely the wrongdoers and their victims, but also those who fail to take notice and thus implicitly become complicit in the wrongdoing, thereby allowing it to multiply. Making this situation explicit is what Cicero did in this long letter to his son—by extension a testimony to the younger generations that would survive the terror Caesar's ambition had unleashed on the Republic and the world. In all the things that we do—the entire realm of our actions, private and public—Cicero asked that men cease to be oblivious of others and become mindful of being seen in public.

Greed and intemperance were the lower forms of self-preservation and pleasure seeking. Basking in the limelight of an orchestrated triumphal march, the circus of hailing the chief, the Caesar propaganda conveniently hid the murders and treachery that made it happen under Rome's authority. The mass men—the yes men—cheered on. Thugs, cheaters and the fools who saw nothing wrong with strong men moved front-and-center of a world in decay yet and in full regalia.

At the conclusion of the second section (Book II) of this work, Cicero warned that all "outward advantages . . . may be weighed against one another: glory, for example, may be preferred to riches, an income derived from city property to one derived from the farm. To this class of comparisons belongs that famous saying of old Cato's: when he was asked what was the most profitable feature of an estate, he replied: 'Raising cattle successfully.' What next to that? 'Raising cattle with fair success.' And next? 'Raising cattle with but slight success.' And fourth? 'Raising crops.' And when his questioner said 'How about money-lending?' Cato replied 'How about murder?'" It is clear the money-lender was seen as the rich man incarnate who would require payment at the cost of life and limb—an assessment that Cato shared with many after him.

How, then, were these ideas treated by Christian scholars and the modern world? The Christian thinker Thomas Aquinas questioned (in *Summa Theologica*, Part II-II, question 25, article 4) whether we should love our neighbor more than ourselves. He interpreted the phrase by Paul of Tarsus (Saint Paul) as meaning that we should seek the common good more than the private one, only because the common good guaranteed the private one by making it consonant with others and a commonality of goals.

By making your personal good—those things and services to our benefit and advantage—a matter of connection with others, you avoid an inevitable downfall, in the exclusive concern with yourself to the detriment of others. Hard-core individualists don't care and can't be bothered—so it seems at first. Yet many uninterested folks will give when pressured, but otherwise they too have to act rationally by prioritizing their activities toward themselves. Positively, there is an ultimate common good—best attainable in connection with God, the source of all goods, private at first, but secondly and more importantly shared and exchanged. "Mine" and "yours" are exchanged freely when the source of the gift is present to the minds of fellows—they are free, reciprocal altruists.

The modern Western world—Christian in outlook and realistic in practice when promoting the common good—is born of the contest between, and complementarity of, the private and public goods. An ethics of responsibility for a world not structured by class (or caste) ethos will be based on the conviction that adhering to a narrow (class, religious or ethnic/tribal) identity works against the ultimate goal of justice, harmony and equality from which no group or religion can take exception. Privileges—the *privatae leges*, or private laws—for individuals, groups or cities will be curtailed, as they are found contrary to the world of scientific or technological innovation of the new entrepreneurs. Nobles have to compete with fortune seekers or "equals," who gamble not at the table but by introducing new products at cheaper prices—thereby breaking the major discrepancies between classes and individuals. Self-discipline and a concern for the consequences of one's actions are counted as virtues of the middle class, worth showing to an entire public—even if it had to be, as in the case of Molière, to the effete French court of Louis XIV.

Adam Smith pointed out that justice is an obligatory virtue to which not one of us can take exception without unleashing the alarm and antagonisms of others. Neighbors come to the rescue of victims and will not be satisfied unless or until the culprits are stopped, neutralized, and punished with the loss of their freedom, or potentially even their lives. A police force and a justice system are the necessary supplements to this immediate assertion of justice as a moral sentiment. There is a second, essential virtue to which Smith called attention: it is beneficence—encompassing charity with monies as well as the volunteering of time and energy for causes benefiting others. This virtue alleviates suffering by empowering individuals to reach goals from which they will benefit. Education and health are seen as the primary targets of such beneficent actions—but in actuality beneficence starts at every level of action—with good will and a positive outlook on our fellow men. Beneficence is a private virtue to be praised, as it has a social function of emulation of communication and sociability. But the essential point is that justice is mandatory whereas beneficence remains optional.

For Kant the role of enlightened citizens—and philosophic jurists —is to promote intellectually compelling ways of relating to others and reflectively inside each one of us individually. The consequences of our no longer being "minors" under the care of "superiors" but of daring to know how and where we stand with respect to each other—these consequences emerge from communication and unhindered exploration of the world. Communication increases our share of the earth, which can happen only if justice enables, but also trumps, beneficence, since justice is universal and beneficence always entails particulars. This pre-eminence of justice over beneficence means that a simple good will constantly influences the idea of yourself as worth as much as any other—just like it influences the idea of the other person as worth as much as yourself. The duty of justice is obligatory, whereas the duty of beneficence is meritorious. The first cannot be avoided, the second must be advocated but not acted upon with unfailing regularity.

Anthropologists and historians will point out that commerce begins with expressions of legality and the pledge of mutual respect regarding reciprocal (yet different) obligations. The legal rationality of the contract prescribes a path that pre-empts the play of self-regarding impulses and ad-hoc rationalizations. In any contract there are negative guidelines of indictment and penalty that guarantee for signatories the desirability of their connection. Kant would agree with anthropologists and historians that legality is the sine qua non of civilization. But there is also morality, and the consequences of dealing with all—others and oneself—in ways that respect our universally desirable freedom.

The value of man is found as an end-in-itself. To have morality is to promote a world where givers give without expectations of an immediate return but because they are treating the other person as someone who should be given assistance—as they themselves would like to be treated. To have morality is to want to commit ourselves to a world where takers take the gift but recognize that in this actual world of limited resources perhaps another person might have needed that gift more urgently than they did. In a rational society we acknowledge our debts to parents, kin and others—and the expression of gratitude on our part amounts to both relief bestowed upon a single individual and a model of action to be emulated by others in a world dominated by self-regard and uncaring.

Having the Golden Rule as a guideline puts us on the path of thinking of others as much as we think of ourselves and of ourselves in the same terms as we think of others—preventing our selfishness or their selfishness from ad hoc rationalizations. Mother Teresa was inspired by the following:

> People are illogical, unreasonable, and self-centered. Love them anyway. If you do good, people will accuse you of selfish ulterior motives. Do good anyway. If you are successful, you will win false friends and true enemies. Succeed anyway. The good you do today will be forgotten tomorrow. Do good anyway. Honesty and frankness make you vulnerable. Be honest and frank anyway. The biggest men and women with the biggest ideas can be shot down by the smallest men and women with the smallest minds. Think big anyway. People favor underdogs but follow only top dogs. Fight for a few underdogs anyway. What you spend years building may be destroyed overnight. Build anyway. People really need help but may attack you if you do help them. Help people anyway. Give the world the best you have and you'll get kicked in the teeth. Give the world the best you have anyway.[3]

In a moral world where individuals treat themselves and others as ends-in-themselves, the thought always exists for this moral person that he or she might not have done all things perfectly, yet did the right things a number of times and stuck with those decisions. The forgotten man as an end-in-itself is either the one that has been repressed and treated as a means to other people's ends, or it is yourself, as you forgot to treat yourself as you would have had to be treated if the world didn't have those obstacles and people unwilling to help you.

Let not the takers appear to be givers, let not the takers endlessly draw you, and others, into a plight where your gifts are forced and you become the facilitators of another age of irresponsibility. Redistributive justice is a misnomer, as William G. Sumner understood so well. Impartial spectators always recognize beneficence, as they will not fail to detect ignorance and foolishness or hypocrisy and deception—in the specifics of our interaction with a world with no lack of deceivers and fools along the way. Just like a crime needs a proper indictment with the specifics of the facts and ascertainable intentions, a beneficent action needs to be circumscribed to a doer and a recipient, with the doer oftentimes trying to remain anonymous. Yet without the two, without the doing and the receiving being acknowledged as acts of good will, the extending of goods and services is transformed into a cycle of dependency and cynicism.

NOTES

1. Since this classic is difficult to find, we want the readers to become aware of a recent reprint: William G. Sumner, *The Forgotten Man, and Other Essays* (Lenox, MA: Hard Press Publishing, 2013)

2. Most of the classic works mentioned in this chapter are readily available in most libraries, and for that reason we will not provide specific references to them. It is only when the work is hard to find, such as the book in the previous endnote, that we will mention how it could be obtained.

3. The Paradoxical Commandments were written by Kent M. Keith as part of his book, *The Silent Revolution: Dynamic Leadership in the Student Council*, published in 1968 by Harvard Student Agencies, Cambridge, Massachusetts. More information is available at www.para doxicalcommandments.com.

Afterword and Summary
in the Form of an Open Letter

Nicolás Sánchez

Dear Readers:

It is my hope that Professor Michael Gendre and I have successfully achieved our main goals for this book: explaining to the public why we face serious political conflicts in America, and how we must deal with them. Politics revolves around a combination of ideologies (derived from philosophical positions), the mindset of citizens, economic policies and institutional arrangements. I sought Michael Gendre's help in the writing of this book because I had little or no background on ideologies and the noneconomic motivations of people, which depend in large part on the ethical norms to which people subscribe. My field of studies is economics, and hence I could contribute on the economic motivations of people, the economic policies of governments and the analysis of institutional arrangements—subjects that constitute my major contributions to academic publishing.

Scholars talk about the importance of interdisciplinary research, yet find it difficult to bring it about. This is not surprising, for each discipline has its own point of view and starting assumptions. In economics, for example, we generally treat the mindset of people as a given, assuming that their preferences are static; this allows economists to make predictions, generally accurate in the short run. Regrettably, those of us who study institutions realize that institutional change comes about in part because personal preferences change: sometimes as the result of the new options that open up as technologies change, sometimes as the result of new ideologies becoming ascendant, and often enough because of effective propaganda promoted by governments.

I needed help in understanding changes in the mindset of people, and Michael Gendre opened up for me a wide and powerful philosophical literature that explained how the world could be conceived from very different perspectives. I thank him immensely for that. With regard to propaganda, the two of us have international backgrounds that allowed us to uncover misleading information the minute we saw and heard it. Michael grew up in French colonial Africa and I grew up in Cuba.

In the end, we found a good guide in the German philosopher Immanuel Kant; he provided us with a constructive mindset that could help us explain the political conflicts that exist in America today. It was said by none other than Albert Einstein that the definition of insanity is doing something over and over again and expecting different results; but Einstein was only partially right in his characterization of insanity. Before people do things, they have attitudes that reflect ethical norms and economic interests. Therefore, people keep doing the same thing over and over again because they fail to challenge their own philosophical beliefs and economic assumptions. We cannot change behaviors unless we change the way people think about themselves and about the world that surrounds them. In a sense, what we have tried to do in this book is to get people to challenge their preconceptions. We did so in a variety of ways.

We have argued that people in power—one, or many, or a vast bureaucracy—try to manipulate the people they govern, for the simple reason that it is in their self-interest to do so. In the old days, rulers could control people because they had exclusive power and control over land, and had the means to coerce people through the use of force. Governance today, of course, still requires the use of force; but people have tried to diffuse government power by dividing it among different branches; these actions have helped to reduce the excessive and arbitrary use of force. Far more important from a modern perspective, however, is that the control of land, and all other assets, can also be diffused by promoting the widespread ownership of private property. When wealth is widely diffused among various sectors of the population, we are able to create a counterbalance to the power of government. Regrettably, when the control of wealth is separated from its ownership (as it has occurred in the last century and a half) those who control capital can form new coalitions with the governing elite and, together, lead countries into disastrous wars.

These ideas are not our own, of course, but people forget the course of history. Tyrannies arise at all times and in all ages. They occur in part because people forget the moral precepts that defended their personal freedoms. In the West, we used to defend personal values grounded in our religious beliefs; this is no longer possible, however, because academic circles have become antireligious. The rise to power of communist ideologies and the Nazi state in the 20th century should have warned us that our personal liberties needed to be independent of our religious traditions. The incredible success of Islamic fundamentalism in the 21st century also demonstrates that even religious traditions can be subverted from within and can support the suppression of freedom.

Hence we must recover other Western traditions that also helped us ground our freedoms. We have disclosed the ideas of the eminent economists who explained the workings of free markets, the ideas of the eminent philosophers who defended personal freedoms, and the ideas of our eminent Founding Fathers, who fought for the creation of an enduring participatory democracy.

Our chapter on bread and circuses is a reminder that governments manipulate us. The chapters on duties remind us that we, as individuals, have the responsibility to take care of ourselves while also taking care of others: we should not abrogate these duties to the government. Our chapters on government organization and performance reminds us that competitive markets reduce, rather than increase, conflicts among people. Governments can help create wealth, under very specific circumstances, but the main source of wealth creation is technical change, which is itself a major source of wealth destruction; therefore, that which makes some of us wealthy makes some of us poor, as technologies change—that is the nature of the world we live in, and not much can be done except to ameliorate the suffering of those who are unable to fend for themselves.

Governments have reinvented themselves as the providers of goods and services for the poor, engaging in widespread redistributional efforts and creating, willfully or not, cultures of dependency (a social pathology). This has been allowed for a variety of reasons. One is that people have lost their altruistic ethic—something that they must recover. Another is that people fail to realize that government policies are not optimal in allocating resources—rather, free and competitive markets are the best means of achieving not just efficiency, but also conflict resolution among divergent interests. Most important of all, people fail to understand the distinction between risk and uncertainty, allowing governments (rather than private institutions by means of insurance) to try to minimize risks, while their true function is to try to minimize uncertainty, a most difficult task which is constantly undermined with arbitrary changes to government policies!

The foundation of government power in our times resides on a deeply held belief; namely, that our main goal in life is the pursuit of happiness, rather the pursuit of self-actualization. Even Thomas Jefferson was wrong in emphasizing the pursuit of happiness as one of our main goals. (The brilliant philosopher Hannah Arendt has noted that "the pursuit of happiness" has been misconstrued to mean the ideals of the nouveau riche, flaunting toys but unwilling to understand the community needs of nations, states and cities.) Contrast the phrase in the Declaration of Independence with that which we advocate: the pursuit of self-actualization. In line with Aristotle, Adam Smith, and Kant we argued that people should try to attain their full potential; and to do so, oftentimes a great deal of sacrifice and unhappiness is indeed required. The consequences of this alternative perspective are novel, and perhaps extremely surprising.

First, the purpose of education is to discover the child's potentials and promote the child's self-actualization. Second, private property rights secure the moral foundations that individuals deserve, since private property rights assist people in reaching their full potential. Third, the lives of people will gain a valid and achievable goal which will provide them not with happiness, but with satisfaction and pride. Fourth, the positive role that government can play in social relations is to provide everyone an egalitarian start in early life and a protective net in old age—plus the caring of people throughout their lives if they are physically or mentally unable to care for themselves. In other words, government redistributional policies take effect at the start and at the end of life, but not during the most productive years of people's lives.

The "pursuit of happiness" is truly a dangerous goal, in the sense that the poor think that money buys happiness and demand to live like the rich, with the assistance of newly created entitlements; and the rich, unaware of their own limitations, become dissatisfied with their own accomplishments. They, too, realize that wealth does not trigger happiness. I often observe that both the poor and the rich commit suicide: proof, if one were needed, that money doesn't buy happiness. In contrast, satisfaction and self-actualization are attainable goals that, at some sacrifice, can be reached by both the poor and the rich. Self-actualization is the true means of empowering people.

We discussed many topics at great length in this book. We explained the rationale for the ethical beliefs that were advocated by Kant, one of the greatest minds that the world and Western civilization ever produced. We defended private property based on ethical norms. We discussed repeatedly the need to limit the power of government, without excluding government from our lives, for government has a role to play in a well-functioning state. We even argued against most forms of inheritance, a position that might appear contrary to the principles that we promoted; however, we demonstrated that those principles require, in fact, significant restrictions on inheritance. We proposed and encouraged the giving away of (taxable) gifts before people become too frail to manage their properties; however, we also accepted that the elderly could retain their wealth in the form of annuities and money holdings if they so desired.

Governments remain powerful to this very day, and especially powerful in this country. Governments have the ability to spy on people and cover up their own misdeeds. Politicians end up being bought once they get to Washington or the state capitals, with funds provided by special interest groups. The federal government has the power to print money and borrow money from abroad, and that needs to be changed. The executive branch ignores Constitutional limitations when it decides to engage in wars. And the Supreme Court has become the arbiter of the elites, rather than the bulwark of our constitutional liberties.

When the time came to assess how the 10th amendment to the U.S. Constitution could be reinvigorated, it became necessary for us to think decidedly outside the box, and propose six constitutional amendments which we fully expected some readers to find "out of season," simply because they had never been proposed before. Indeed, they required an open mind from readers.

We have enjoyed demonstrating to readers that we do not have a conservative or liberal bias, arguing on the one hand for limited government and on the other for limiting inheritance. Our bias against searching for happiness must have upset those who call themselves Libertarians, who in turn must have been delighted with our approach to the money supply.

One final topic required scrutiny: Imperialism. We argued that the expansion of government powers and the control of America by a self-serving elite have been leading us to imperialistic policies for many decades now. Imperialism is a passé topic in academia, but it needs to be reevaluated by the public at large.

We wrote this book, then, as both a Wake UP Call and a Call to Action. We are willing to defend these arguments here, there and everywhere because we truly believe in what we say. Feel free to contact me via email at nicolas.sanchez@aol.com, and I will respond to you. I am devoting my retirement years to the ideas which we have expressed in this book.

Appendix A

Our Assumptions

It often happens that after reading a book, pamphlet or article the reader concludes that even though the arguments seem plausible, he or she cannot internalize them—meaning that the reader cannot make them part of his or her own mindset, let alone practice the consequences or implications of those arguments. The reasons for this behavior are not even clear to the reader. When the person thinks hard enough about his or her reluctance, the discovery is usually made that the writers' assumptions are different from those held by the reader.

Therefore, the two authors of this book want to make explicit their assumptions, to save the reader's time. We begin with the idea that our democratic process (and the institutional arrangements in which this process evolves) is not working. This can be defended by pointing out that electoral participation at all levels of government has fallen dramatically over the years. Most people want to distance themselves from politics and view politicians as self-serving (at best) or simply as crooks. Yet, we believe that our democratic process is worth saving, but something radical needs to be done.

A democracy, of course, offers a well-defined governance structure. In America, this is characterized by the separation of powers within the federal government, and between the states and the national government. Both of these separations require a balancing act, and there is no doubt that this balance has been skewed significantly in favor of the national (or federal) government and its executive branch. We share this assumption with most students of our American Constitution, who conclude that the balance can be restored only when we limit the size of the federal government and give greater power to the states.

We have made explicit proposals in that regard. However, such a balancing act is not enough. For we believe that even if we were to achieve an ideal governance structure in America, if people did not change their ethical values—which impact the way they think about what the government could and should accomplish—then our governing process cannot serve us well through our historical journey. Let us explain.

As a nation, we live in a highly competitive world, and if America fails to increase its wealth and its human resources, it is inevitable that others (who do not share our democratic values) will surpass our country in intellectual achievement and economic power: this will put our nation in peril. The argument behind this book (and we recognize that it is only an argument, not a proven fact) is that we need to return to the Kantian values that prevailed in Western Europe through a good part of the nineteenth century. (Regrettably, Kant's ethical ideas were obscured and made a mockery by European imperialism and the writings of Karl Marx and others). These values emphasize self-improvement and self-actualization, and on treating others as ends and not as means.

We hold that, as a nation, we have to stress both self-actualization and the duty to treat others the way we want others to treat us. These goals require a strong defense of private property and competitive markets, while simultaneously providing a reasonably equal start in the life of young people, and a reasonable safety net for people in old age. We have a duty to help others who cannot help themselves (the young, the old, and by extension the infirm) but others also have a duty to not place undue financial burdens on those who, in their middle years (from 18 to 78), are trying to achieve vigorously their own self-improvement and self-actualization. The culture of dependency (except where dependency is a natural condition among the young, the old and the infirm) must come to an end.

Now, someone may argue that our educational system has, implicitly at least, the same goals that we are expressing here and throughout the book. We deny that. Our schools do not teach values: our schools teach a mishmash of various forms of propaganda. The Kantian agenda is based on arguments about the worth of individuals as rational human beings, who deserve to be treated as ends and not as means. The Kantian agenda places an emphasis on self-actualization and the unique contributions that people can make to the economy and the polis. Our schools sometimes encourage behaviors that help achieve those goals, but never do they explain the *reasons* behind those goals.

Our schools promote the delusion that government intervention provides the means of solving all of our social problems. People forget the basic fact that government officials are more often than not self-serving and help promote vested interests, which are seeking massive income redistribution to help themselves. We are not against income redistribution per se, if and when it is appropriate within our value scheme and if it can be morally justified. Our proposal to limit and tax inheritance (or to be more exact, to tax gifts from an older generation to a younger generation) demonstrates that. The problem is that our schools have ceased to teach how governments in the past have oppressed citizens; or even when they do so, will promote the idea that somehow our *current* government is different. In other words, our schools fail to teach a *theory* about how governments operate. If the reader is looking for such a theory, it can be found in the writings of what is called "public choice theory" within the economics field—with many economists winning the Nobel Prize for the work they have contributed to that field.

There is also a widespread ignorance today about how older generations succeeded and failed in handling the problems that they faced. Their strategies were dependent on the values which they held. We have proudly recounted the history of the ideas that have taken us to where we are today. Prior generations were informed by the Judeo-Christian traditions prevailing in their schools. That tradition, rightly or wrongly, has been pushed to the sidelines. The 20th century saw the establishment of governments that consciously sought to eliminate those Judeo-Christian values, allowing for the growth of evil in Russia, Germany and many other countries of the world.

Times are beginning to change and we are aware of some religious revival at work in China, Latin America, Africa and perhaps even in the rich countries of North America and Europe; still, no theology is going to be the handmaid of politics in the modern world. The ethical teachings of Kant, on the other hand, can be absorbed within a secular political environment, and they are compatible with Judeo-Christian values. But another point about Kant needs to be made.

To some, Kant does not appear to move along the same line of thinking as the American Founding Fathers and their British Whig forebears. Our response is twofold. First, at the anecdotal level, Kant's family was from Scottish stock and his moral outlook strongly reminds many readers of the Puritans' work ethic and their devotion to a good will. But far more important is that in Kant's work the individual is defined by a primordial "mine," to which corresponds a primordial "yours" (and a primordial "his" and "hers") from which commerce and business intercourse arise. We grant that this notation is not developed into anything else but a paragraph in the "Doctrine of Right," which was part of his book *The Metaphysics of Morals*, but it is crucial in the development of our own arguments.

Kant's perspective is in high confluence with John Locke and the rest of the American Founding Fathers. When it comes to governance, we were pleased to repeat in our text the famous Kennedy quote "Ask not what your country can do for you, ask what you can do for your country;" yet we assert that this is not enough. Yes, we need a sense of duty towards our country, but we also need a sense of duty towards others, which can contribute to the vast majority of citizens achieving their own self-actualization. President Kennedy's quote is memorable, yet it is also incomplete because it failed to explain *why* he held those beliefs.

We hope, then, that this appendix helps the reader to understand our assumptions and the goals that guide our writings. The reader must now reflect on his and her assumptions, and determine which of those are in contradiction with ours. If there is no contradiction, we hope the reader can internalize and act on the beliefs that we promote.

Appendix B

Our Understanding of Scholarship

A scholar is someone who has the ability—in terms of time and independence—and also the interest and credentials to research, discover, and publicize what is the case. The task of the scholar is to find the truth by dismantling the scaffoldings of falsehoods or mere disorganized opinions. At the outset of opening a book, or deciding to spend more time researching a line of thought, it is necessarily to ask a simple set of questions regarding the credentialed individuals who write or profess to know better: Do these writers or scholars raise issues and questions? Do they provide answers (or hypotheses)? Do they promote novelty in understanding while maintaining dispassion from all specific political or business points of views? Or, are these persons scratching the surface of research and providing a gloss with the intent of promoting their careers and professional affiliations?

In this book, we the two authors have given positive answers to the first three questions, within the context of an ethics of responsibility—which is different from an ethics of mere loyalty and conviction. The two of us are also well-established scholars, with no need to promote our careers or professional affiliations. What we do in this appendix is to sketch out how our approach opens up a better critical understanding of the world of scholarship.

We raise another question. If absolute truth is elusive (and only God has it, while we are capable at most of *docta ignorantia* or learned ignorance), how do scholars reach the best view? They have (1) to navigate a sea of facts; (2) to sort out, classify, summarize opinions, and (3) to attempt to extract the proper criteria, issue criticisms and articulate new valid hypotheses amidst change or uncertainties. Also, scholars need the time to explore at their leisure, together with some level of freedom, the recognized paths of prior scholarship.

It is a hackneyed notation going back to the Greeks and Cicero (the great scholar, orator and politician of Roman times) that all too often "scholars" are specialists, and narrow specialists at that, of a certain topic in their field. Many things turn out simply unknown and unfamiliar to the individual scholar, and so we witness that the multi-disciplinary credo many profess to adhere to is empty talk. Here we see in just a nutshell the paradox of the individual scholar: on the one hand, he or she is confined in (and somewhat prisoner of) the past making its way into the present; yet the scholar also wants to make a difference within the future of his or her field, or even of different fields.

Would Marie Curie (the French renown physicist and chemist) have known that X-rays would revolutionize medicine, astronomy and astrophysics? Would she have known that geophysics would revolutionize our current understanding of anthropology? One is inclined to answer no, and yet she did. If we consider the case of scientific research, specifically in the hard sciences, new fields open up by the process of invalidation of earlier theories (and paradigms) and the discovery of new phenomena. The scholar and the researcher produce new understanding of facts that can be shown to take place, and he or she produces new "techniques" enabling other researchers—and on their heels, industry—to offer discoveries, which translate into products and services that up until then could not be even imagined.

Consider the example of wireless radio, and the major impact it had on the world between the two world wars; consider the role the transistor had in starting space exploration, putting a few men on the moon, and in increasing the standard of living of countless individuals in the boom years after WWII. Finally, consider the computer chip which can now pack the power of enormous resources within the thin walls of a cellular phone. No one could have imagined the impact of wireless radio from a consideration of the telegraph or wireless Morse messaging.

Qualitative leaps being made by scientific discoveries are the handmaidens of technology that benefits the masses, and lead to more research. The intelligent observers and risk takers—i.e., the entrepreneurs—are the ones pushing utility to its ultimate goal, being of service to the greatest numbers at the lowest cost; yet they themselves understand the foremost need to exert their own imaginations beyond the current state of affairs.

But what about scholarship in the humanities and the social sciences, including economics? To be sure, the same paradox obtains: the credentialed scholar has a definite sense of the past making its way into the present, and would like to make discoveries that will create a difference for the future of the field. But there is something different in these fields: it is the conviction of a certain inevitability of past mistakes, errors, or illusions that will repeat themselves in an unreformed future. To be sure, some will argue—and we concur—that the sought innovations will certainly undercut the inevitability of these mistakes.

William Faulkner made the reflection, which arguably is ambivalent—that "the past is never dead, in fact it is not even past." Hence we face a contradiction between two beliefs that are themselves reasonable: (a) on the side of pessimism, Faulkner's words indicate that human minds are inevitably pulled into ruts and fallacies from which they can hardly extricate easily; and (b) on the side of optimism, this means that there is a lasting effect of the past in both the evolution of the species and in the course of the human adventure on earth.

Thinking of our own modern times, we all know of the thrill and excitement of novelties that punctuate our own age of discovery. The reader needs to remind himself or herself that in the past one hundred years we have witnessed dramatic changes not only in our material culture, but also in our ideals, social environment and institutions. But how can this change be grasped and understood? The average person feels overwhelmed by the specialists, who oftentimes provide contradictory messages, deeply dependent upon the disciplines from which they come. Typically, books read by the common man or woman have a single point of view.

Our scholarship is different because it is the collaboration of two persons with backgrounds in both the humanities and the social sciences, who have made a conscious effort to understand each other's points of view. We have made an effort to become generalists rather than specialists when it comes to arguments, in order to be understood by readers, without ignoring the professional training that each of us has received. There is nothing utterly novel here: In an important way, innovative scholars have to be open to different ways of thinking, becoming generalists and even at times classicists.

Kant, the great German philosopher, notoriously said that subsequent readers, specifically commentators and scholars, may claim that they understand an original author better than the author understood himself or herself: "It is by no means unusual upon comparing the thoughts which an author has expressed in regard to his subject, whether in ordinary conversation or in writing, to find that we understand better than he has understood himself. As he has not sufficiently determined his concept, he has sometimes spoken, or even thought, in opposition to his own intentions." (*Critique of Pure Reason*.) Yet, at the same time, Kant argued that there is a tendency of the daring mind of scholars to claim that they finally reached an absolute. Hence, a critical thinker has to question the scholars' conclusions and show them to be hypotheses and partial answers.

This idea of checking a view objectively—both sympathetically and critically beyond its point of inception—is something both Socrates and Kant pursued for the benefit of the common man, and it is at the core of the culture of the Greek democratic system, which we inherited from them. We urge our readers to do the same.

Socrates was one of the first to expose his ideas in open public spaces, which we now call the marketplace of ideas; he discovered the tendency of some men to hold certain ear-catching notions, which under serious questioning they cannot defend. These were the politicians (and their helpers, the rhetoricians and sophists) as well as the poets. Notoriously, too, in his trial for corruption of the youth, Socrates received a guilty verdict and the death sentence. And many noted that he didn't hurl at his accusers the moral category of evil-doing. Rather he saw stubbornness and hubris (excessive ego) emerging from the accusers' flawed understanding of things.

It was then Socrates' mission—which he had no option but to accept in the wake of an oracle passed at Delphi—to expose that no superior wisdom was owned by anybody in Greece. He repeatedly explained that his doubts about such superior wisdom came not from some sort of enjoyment of his in seeking antagonisms, but came in fact from the same source that encouraged him forward (for the sake of the next generation) to analyze and parse the words and analyze the lofty claims of the front row of the Greek contemporaries. This, he claimed, was the proper use of our reasoning power and logical thinking.

Aristotle recognized the tendency of discourse to slip into fallacies where the meanings or uses of terms are extended to the point where a conclusion is forced—a conclusion that wouldn't have been drawn if the terms had been properly defined or the connections of ideas more carefully established. Sloppy expression and inaccurate relations lead to an invalid conclusion. In this connection we hear often praise of the English empiricists, especially Locke and Hume, for reiterating the same Aristotelian caveats in the English language.

Still, today as in days past, the power to impress the average person may continue if the writer's far-flung presentations are uninterrupted, unchecked and unopposed. The average person often realizes that this is our lot when dealing with politicians, and nearly always the case in dealing with literary authors and commentators. So this age of ours is not so different from the age of classical Greece—its glory and its shortcomings are the same, although under a different type of language.

The marketplace of ideas can and need to be full of opposites—yet these opposites need to clash. Relativism often starts off debate. That even happens when the anthropologist, whose professional business (and even ethics) needs to abstain from moral judgment on practices deeply offensive to his or her convictions. In the marketplace of ideas, the empire of free trade demands that contracts must be honored, and urbanity be adhered to. Yet even anthropology evolves because new facts are adduced, new hypotheses are ventured, new experiences are gained by the many who either do not have the inclination to pursue them or think it's not worth trying—all occurring in the midst of a pool of thinkers interested in the acquisition of partial (but never absolute) knowledge.

Scholarship, then, is the ability to recognize a proper connection between particulars and more general elements, by pointing out improper connections. Probing scholarship must have breadth and scope as well as focus—this means a wide array of context and reference points. Regrettably, when we look at recent philosophers, it's hard not to be struck by the existential pose, the Romantic allure, the nearly certain ego problems that fester underneath the surface—all the more striking when those individuals have great intellectual stamina.

Kant, of course, is beyond reproach here. And so is one of his immediate successors, Arthur Schopenhauer, who could see that the entire intellectual elites of Germany were living a life of self-deception, with endless and pointless strivings for glory. Schopenhauer recommended the "will not-to-will," in order to take care of that major problem among Europeans of his time. But, whether Schopenhauer fully realized it or not, the ideal of self-effacement and denial fell flat on its face when novelties were produced aplenty by the will of his contemporaries.

Hence the ego or the "self" returned with a vengeance with philosophers such as Nietzsche, Heidegger and Wittgenstein. Those three, and their countless followers, are clearly central to the philosophical establishment today in most European and American universities and colleges. And it is striking that for all three, the thinking activity is so powerful in creating its own terms, paradigms and vistas on two millennia of Western philosophy, that they all claimed to be thinking beyond good and evil. Their experiment in philosophy failed.

We were partially inspired by Hannah Arendt, but didn't follow her completely. An interesting issue arose in the process of writing these pieces—as well as during several presentations made to students in Massachusetts—as we were reading and drawing the meaning of classical texts. The issue was the need to restore an ethics of responsibility, which became tied together with the essential notion of institutional arrangements upon which we both agreed to work.

Not surprisingly, education loomed large but also issues of ownership arose, and we both decided to discuss them at length in our book. It is our hope that the Kantian ideas that we adopted as a guide serve to inspire the readers in achieving more productive and satisfactory lives. We conclude that the meaning of true scholarship is not disconnected from a full embrace of psychology, economics, history, philosophy and all the arts (from rhetoric to forensics). We hope that our readers will have the leisure to experience works or productions that include our own book, and that they recommend the same to others, which in turn stimulates a striving for excellence in the new generation of scholars, writers, even artists and performers.

Appendix C

The Kantian Texts and Their Context

Our approach to Kant is premised on the superiority of the will (being guided by principles of practical philosophy, as explained in the two texts *The Grounding for the Metaphysics of Morals*[1] and the *Critique of Practical Reason*[2] over the other two faculties of the soul, i.e., the cognitive faculty and the capacity to experience pleasure and displeasure. Willing is higher than knowing on two accounts: (a) the *Critique of Pure Reason*[3] established that our cognitive abilities cannot reach unconditional objects because in cognition and knowledge everything depends on sensibility and logical connections working together; and (b) because willing starts from freedom, which is an unconditional element, not dependent on an immediate concern for happiness of self and others—in other words, willing accepts displeasure and doesn't always count pleasures as a good.

According to the *Critique of Pure Reason*, our cognitive abilities must be restricted from the unconditional tendencies of metaphysics—where ideas refer to absolute realities beyond the known entities of the physical or psychological worlds. But this restriction does not apply to the will and our practical abilities. As soon as we enter freedom, we categorically assert the supremacy of a duty applicable to all rational beings. Validation does not come from our experiencing empirical realities; instead, the validation of our thoughts and unfolding commitment to a good will originates in the call of freedom. The validation of the will is higher than dealing with competing incentives. Also, the validation of the good will—and its moral duties—is independent from mystical aspirations to perfection never accessible to us, but known only to God. The individual must own the original fact that, with his or her action, freedom is in his or her care, and through that agency alone, he or she is in the position of making decisive contributions to a well-organized society of rational creatures.

By standing as a legislator in the human world order—rather than as an observer amidst nature—the agent is granted a place with duties and responsibilities. As creatures endowed with practical reason, we conceive of society as a focus for reason committed to act; and we conceive of our actions as affecting the unfolding of history.

Kant first presents ethical guidelines for his moral ideas in the *Grounding for the Metaphysics of Morals*. This popular text prepares the way for the more theoretical considerations of the second critique, the *Critique of Practical Reason*. A major proposition of that second work is that no "highest good" can be defined without the first mention of, and reliance upon, duty and the categorical imperative, because an individual who is a legislator must think for *all* rational beings.

We now need to consider the *Metaphysics of Morals*,[4] with its two parts: the "Doctrine of Right" and the "Doctrine of Virtue." We followed several themes and propositions from the "Doctrine of Right," especially regarding the unsurpassable nature of definite things that at the outset are to be "mine" or "yours," for it is from our various relations to such things (and to the agency of others) that the doctrine of right emerges. We also took notice of Kant's work on judgment, the *Critique of Judgment*,[5] which explores the pure judgment of taste on the beautiful and the sublime. In his *Anthropology from a Pragmatic Point of View*,[6] Kant had combined the need for the development of our cognitive faculty, of pleasure and displeasure, as well as of the faculty of desire—he had defined pragmatically education and human self-actualization in relation to a world of knowledge and social exchange.

Several of Kant's political writings spell out his understanding of the body politic as a "republic," in the care of "moral politicians," whose main concern is to secure freedom and to prevent tyranny and absolutism. Such an interest in moral politicians is tantamount to seeking an alignment of ethics and politics, and the pursuance of values that enhance civic awareness and sound moral education. Three authors with a known interest in Kant's classical liberalism and constitutionalism steered us toward articulating the juncture between ethics and politics: Ernst Cassirer, Karl Jaspers, and Hannah Arendt. Each deserves an independent subsection.

A. ERNST CASSIRER (1874–1945)

We borrow Cassirer's insistence on the symbolic function of concepts in Kant, and their need to be referred to experience. Concepts are not static; they are not akin to settled definitions, but involve a rule for thinking a multiplicity of cases and lead to the progress of the mind. Cassirer explains that in Kant's view concepts combine an abstract synthesis and a selection of cases and instances, which need to be correlated. This could also apply to ethical and pragmatic concepts, which should be referred to a multiplicity of cases and instances (e.g., for rational autonomy, social independence, happiness through self-actualization) in order to make the ideas and recommendations capable of eliciting a response—from students or readers generally, whether active scholars or the interested public.

By seeking to expand and diversify the context for the value of the categorical imperative and align this value with politics, we claim that we are in line with Cassirer's acceptance of Kant's philosophy—we only draw more deliberately than he does from jurisdiction, politics, policies, anthropology, history, economics, sociology, linguistics and ethnology. But we point out that Kant suggests in the "Doctrine of Right" that his writing is not merely intended to students of political philosophy but also "philosophic jurists."

The age of the Enlightenment meant to concentrate and dedicate the energies of thinkers to a potentially revolutionary reform of the civil/social state. The thinker most sensitive to this task before Kant was Rousseau: Rousseau wanted "to transform the present improvised form of the state into a rational state; and to change society from a product of blind necessity to one of freedom." Cassirer comments that

> It was not a moral inclination Rousseau had tried to show in his *Discourse on Inequality* that caused man to make the transition from the natural to the social state; . . . more likely man fell victim of society as a result of inexorable fate, by the physical compulsion of external nature, and by the power of his emotions and passions . . . This depraved condition is to be abolished. Man is to return to his original condition and to his original nature; not in order to remain there, but in order from this starting point to build up his social existence all over again. And this time he shall not succumb to the power of his appetites and passions but he shall himself choose and direct. He shall grasp the helm himself and determine both his course and destination. He must know where he is going and why, because *only with this knowledge can he be sure of victory and the final realization of the idea of law* (emphasis added).[7]

Rousseau then could open the way to the secular, revolutionary world we inhabit. Kant certainly sensed it, and a good indication of how Kant's philosophy reacted to the evils of revolutions is given by Karl Jaspers, whose work is discussed below.

B. KARL JASPERS (1883–1969)

More than Cassirer, Jaspers sought to expand the culture of modern men by seeking communication with the cultural achievements from the Western past as well as with important Eastern insights. Experiences of all-encompassing boundaries and connections—life, birth, pain, joy, thinking, action, harmony within the superior power of nature, and death—punctuate the absolutes of beginning, ending, and of a time that endures through human striving.

Jaspers has an assessment of the German contribution to culture by reference to Kant's philosophy, its cosmopolitan ideals and pragmatic anthropology. His book on Kant contains a series of sections under the heading "The Idea of Civil Society" in which he describes and analyzes the republican order, happiness and the law, tyranny and rebellion, war and peace, and the importance of a philosophy of history for human action. He adds that "Kant's philosophy goes counter to the totalizations that began with the systems of German idealism and led by way of Marxism to the practice of total knowledge and total planning."[8]

Countering those tendencies toward despotism, Jaspers follows Kant in highlighting a contrast between happiness and government:

> In a republican order, 'each man pursues his own happiness and every citizen is free to enter into dealings with every other citizen. It is not the function of government to relieve the private person of this concern.' The determining principle of a republican society is not happiness but right ([i.e.,] justice). The principle of right is conceived as social contract. The 'public is equivalent to the legal constitution which, by means of laws, secures the freedom of every man. A civil society cannot be grounded on 'men's ever varying notion of what constitutes their happiness'.[9]

In such a society, rather, each man is free to form his own conception of happiness. Even if the principle of happiness is put forward in good faith, its consequences are disastrous for the ruler and the ruled. Jaspers quotes Kant directly: "The sovereign wishes to make the people happy in his own way and becomes a despot; the people are unwilling to forgo the universal human claim to determine their own happiness and become rebellious." [10]

C. HANNAH ARENDT (1906–1975)

As a scholar of totalitarianism Arendt sought to understand the collapse of traditional morality and formal, constitutional protections in the unfolding history of the totalitarian regimes of the modern world. In *The Human Condition*,[11] she traced that collapse to the reduction of active life to the monopoly of modern labor (while active life was in times past structured hierarchically, included the mastery of work, and made room for the uniqueness of individual/collective actions) and to the demotion of the thinking activity to a subservient capacity.

Individuals were made superfluous in the traumatic experiences of war and economic catastrophe spreading world alienation and disinterest in the common world. Moral values of respect of others—friends, family, and neighbors—collapsed. The mass ideology (the pathology of the scapegoat) could only grow by disaggregating the previous normal restraints in facing adversity and by aggregating violence against others viewed as necessarily hostile. This mentality would forcibly enroll masses of people into collective action, and then only leave them unable to think on their own—as they can become agents or facilitators of murderous criminality against innocents.

Arendt's work began to relate to Kant after the turn caused in her work and teaching career by the capture of Adolf Eichmann, the chief enforcer of Hitler's "Final Solution." In 1960 the Mossad, the Israeli Secret Service, captured Eichmann hiding in plain sight in Argentina and brought him to trial in Jerusalem, where Arendt traveled to document the event. A polemic erupted around her account and assessment in her book *Eichmann in Jerusalem: A Report on the Banality of Evil.* [12] It was her view that Eichmann's role in taking the lead in the extermination of the European Jewry enforced the bureaucratic line of race purity by means made possible by imperialistic and bureaucratic expansion. The greatest crimes are possible when judgments of life and death over individuals are rendered without allowing them the right to speak, defend themselves, or escape their tormenters even for ransom. The ability to act out evil on the part of these tormenters is made possible when absolute, unrestricted power is concentrated in the hands of the supreme leader—and no opposition, challenge, and defense have any chance of standing against the total control of the bureaucratic machine.

The ability to act publicly and in concert with our peers is prepared by judgment and comparative assessments. In *On Revolution,* [13] Arendt studied the contrast between the successful founding of the American Republic and the pathos and failure of the revolution in France, which became mired in the impossible task of ending misery.

It is well known to her readers that Arendt is indebted to two versions of judgment, one connected with action and the second with reflective assessments. While Arendt never sought to define morality on its own (except as the acceptance of the Mosaic Law), the emergence of totalitarianism forced her to seek recognition of the modern inhumanity and depravity not only by factually stating deeds, but through the assessment of such deeds by a spectator who represents to himself or herself a whole story. Re-presentation of a something—of phenomena beyond the grasp of a concept—for the sake of weighing certain matters as tasteful or distasteful was the criterion Kant had formulated for aesthetic judgment.

It was such a form that Arendt saw fit for inclusion in political philosophy, on the border of ethics. She also highlighted in her *Lectures on Kant's Political Philosophy* [14] the belonging together of higher emotions, experiences, and thought experiments (regarding different points of view) that unite rational beings into a thoughtful public and community. She increased our awareness of the "enlarged mentality"—which can voice sorrow and show aversion to apathy—without which our pragmatic anthropology would be either blind (although it can hear the sounds) or deaf (although it can distinguish the actors)—in either case lacking in contact with reality and in the ability to understand what took place or is about to take place.

NOTES

1. Immanuel Kant, *Grounding for the Metaphysics of Morals*, trans. James W. Ellington (Indianapolis: Hackett Publishing Company, 1982).

2. Immanuel Kant, *The Critique of Practical Reason*, trans. Lewis White Beck (New York: Macmillan Publishing Company, 1956).

3. Immanuel Kant, *The Critique of Pure Reason,* trans. Norman Kemp Smith (New York: St Martin's Press, 1965).

4. Immanuel Kant, *Metaphysics of Morals*, trans. and ed. Mary J. Gregor (New York: Cambridge University Press, 1996).

5. Immanuel Kant, *The Critique of Judgment*, trans. Werner S. Pluhar (Indianapolis: Hackett Publishing Company, 1987).

6. Immanuel Kant, *Anthropology from a Pragmatic Point of View*, trans. Victor Lyle Dowdell, (Carbondale and Edwardsville: Southern Illinois University Press, 1978).

7. Ernst Cassirer, *The Philosophy of the Enlightenment,* trans. Fritz C. A. Koelln and James P. Pettegrove (Princeton, N.J.: Princeton University Press, trans., 195), 272.

8. Karl Jaspers, *Kant*, ed. Hannah Arendt, trans. Ralph Manheim (New York: Harcourt, Brace and World, 1962), 110–120.

9. Ibid., p. 111.

10. Ibid., p.112.

11. Hannah Arendt, *The Human Condition* (Chicago: University of Chicago Press, 1958).

12. Hannah Arendt, *Eichmann in Jerusalem: A Report on the Banality of Evil* (New York: Penguin Classics, 1963).

13. Hannah Arendt, *On Revolution* (London: Penguin Books Limited, 1963).

14. Hannah Arendt, *Lectures on Kant's Political Philosophy* (Chicago: Chicago University Press, 1982).

Bibliography

Aquinas, Thomas. *Summa Theologica*, trans. Fathers of the English Dominican Province (Westminster, MD: Christian Classics, 1981).

Arendt, Hannah. *Eichmann in Jerusalem: A Report on the Banality of Evil* (New York: Penguin Classics, 1963).

―――. *Lectures on Kant's Political Philosophy* (Chicago: Chicago University Press, 1982).

―――. *On Revolution* (London: Penguin Books Limited, 1963).

―――. *The Human Condition* (Chicago: University of Chicago Press, 1958).

―――. *The Origins of Totalitarianism* (Orlando, FL: A Harvest Book, 1985).

Aristotle, *Nicomachean ethics*, 2nd ed., trans. Terence Irwin (Indianapolis, IN: Hackett Publishing Company, 1999).

―――. *The Politics*, trans. T. A. Sinclair (London: Penguin Classics, 1962).

Baade, Robert A., Robert Baumann and Victor Matheson, "Selling the Game: Estimating the Economic Impact of Professional Sports through Taxable Sales," *Southern Economic Journal* 74, no. 3 (2008):794-810.

Ballor, Jordan J. "Lord Acton on Catholic and Modern Views of Liberty," last modified on July 17, 2013, accessed October 19, 2015, http://blog.acton.org/archives/57615-lord-acton-on-catholic-and-modern-views-of-liberty.html.

Bendix, Peter. "A History of Baseball's Antitrust Exemption," last updated Dec. 3, 2008, accessed Oct. 30, 2015, http://www.beyondtheboxscore.com/2008/12/3/678134/the-history-of-baseball-s.

Bonachea, Ramon L. and Marta San Martin, *The Cuban Insurrection, 1952-1959* (New Brunswick, NJ: Transaction Publishers, 1974).

Calomiris, Charles W. and Stephen H. Haber, *Fragile by Design* (Princeton University Press, 2014), 216-226.

Cassirer, Ernst. *The Philosophy of the Enlightenment,* trans. Fritz C. A. Koelln and James P. Pettegrove (Princeton, N.J.: Princeton University Press, trans., 195).

Central Intelligence Agency, *The World Factbook*, available at https://www.cia.gov/library/publications/resources/the-world-factbook/.

Cicero, *On Obligations*, trans. P. G. Walsh, (Oxford: Oxford University Press, 2008).

D'Souza, Dinesh. *America: Imagine A World Without Her* (Washington, DC: Regnery Publishing, 2014).

Ferguson, Niall. *Colossus: The Rise and Fall of the American Empire* (New York: Penguin Books, 2004).

―――. *Empire: The Rise and Demise of the British World Order and the Lessons for Global Power* (New York: Basic Books, 2004).

Gallagher, John and Ronald Robinson, "The Imperialism of Free Trade," *The Economic History Review* 6, no. 1 (August 1953): 1–15.

Gigerenzer, *Gerd. Risk Savvy; How to Make Good Decisions* (New York: Viking, 2014).

Glenza, Jessica. "Netflix launches $7.99 service for Cuba despite average wage of $17 a month." *The Guardian*, February 9, 2015.

Hannan, Daniel. *Inventing Freedom: How the English-Speaking Peoples Made the Modern World* (London: Broadside Books, 2013).

Henderson, David R. ed. *The Concise Encyclopedia of Economics,* http://www.econlib.org/library/CEE.html.

Hesiod. Works and Days, trans. Hugh Evelyn White, accessed October 20, 2015, http://www.sacred-texts.com/cla/hesiod/works.htm.

Jaspers, Karl. *Kant*, ed. Hannah Arendt, trans. Ralph Manheim (New York: Harcourt, Brace and World, 1962).

Kant, Immanuel. *Anthropology from a Pragmatic Point of View*, trans. Victor Lyle Dowdell, (Carbondale and Edwardsville: Southern Illinois University Press, 1978).

————. *Grounding for the Metaphysics of Morals*, trans. James W. Ellington (Indianapolis: Hackett Publishing Company, 1982).

————. *Metaphysics of Morals*, trans. and ed. Mary J. Gregor (New York: Cambridge University Press, 1996).

————. *Political Writings*, ed. Hans Reiss, trans., H. B. Nisbet (Cambridge, UK: Cambridge University Press, 1991).

————. *The Critique of Judgment*, trans. Werner S. Pluhar (Indianapolis: Hackett Publishing Company, 1987).

————. *The Critique of Practical Reason*, trans. Lewis White Beck (New York: Macmillan Publishing Company, 1956).

————. *The Critique of Pure Reason,* trans. Norman Kemp Smith (New York: St Martin's Press, 1965).

Keith, Kent M. "Do It Anyway," accessed October 20, 2015, http://prayerfoundation.org/mother_teresa_do_it_anyway.htm.

Kendall, Brent. "Supreme Court on Deck in MLB Antitrust Battle? *The Wall Street Journal*, Last updated January 15, 2015, accessed October 30, 2015, http://www.wsj.com/articles/baseballs-antitrust-exemption-upheld-in-appeals-court-1421347744.

King Jr., Martin Luther. "Letter from Birmingham Jail," *The Atlantic*, vol. 212, no. 2, 78-88.

Machiavelli, Niccolo. *The Discourses,* trans. Leslie J. Walker, S.J. (London: Penguin Classics, reprinted 1998).

MacIntyre, Alasdair. *After Virtue: A Study in Moral Theory*, 3^d ed. (Notre Dame, Indiana: University of Notre Dame Press, 2007).

Madison, James, Alexander Hamilton and John Jay. *The Federalist Papers* (New York: Tribeca Books, 2010).

Miles, Richard. *Carthage Must Be Destroyed: The Rise and Fall of an Ancient Civilization* (New York: Viking Press, 2012).

Moyo, Dambisa. "Dead Aid: Why Aid Is Not Working and How There Is a Better Way for Africa (New York: Farrar, Straus and Giroux, 2009).

Park, Sang Mi. "The Paradox of Postcolonial Korean Nationalism: State-Sponsored Cultural Policy in South Korea, 1965-Present," *The Journal of Korean Studies* 15, no.1 (2010): 67-93.

Perez Jr., Louis A. *On Becoming Cuban: Identity, Nationality and Culture* (Chapel Hill: University of North Carolina Press, 1999).

Rothbard, Murray N. *Classical Economics, An Austrian Perspective on the History of Economic Thought, vol 2* (Auburn, Alabama: Ludwig von Mises Institute, 2006).

Roche III, George Charles. "Frédéric Bastiat: A Man Alone," last modified Oct. 20, 2009, accessed Oct. 24, 2015, https://mises.org/library/fr%C3%A9d%C3%A9ric-bastiat-man-alone.

Romo, Ricardo. "Responses to Mexican Immigration, 1910-1930," in ed. Michael R. Ornelas, *Beyond 1848; Readings in the Modern Chicano Historical Experience* (Dubuque, IA: Kendall Hunt Publishing, 1999).

Rosen, Stanley. *The Ancients and the Moderns; Rethinking Modernity* (New Haven, CT: Yale University Press, 1989).

Rucker, Walter C. and James N. Upton, editors, *Encyclopedia of American Race Riots*. 2 vols. (Westport, CT: Greenwood Press, 2006).

Sánchez, Nicolás "Taxation Levels in Cuba and Other Topics of Rhetorical Interests," *Cuba in Transition*, 13 (August 2003): 103-114.

Sánchez, Nicolás, Christopher Kopp and Francis Sanzari. *Destined for Failure: American Prosperity in the Age of Bailouts* (Santa Barbara, CA: Praeger, 2010).

Shikwati, James. "For God's Sake, Please Stop the Aid!" Spiegel Interview with African Economics Expert, August 27, 2005, http://www.spiegel.de/international/spiegel/spiegel-interview-with-african-economics-expert-for-god-s-sake-please-stop-the-aid-a-363663.html.

Sumner, William. *The Forgotten Man, and Other Essays* (Lenox, MA: Hard Press Publishing, 2013).

Thucydides. *History of the Peloponnesian War*, trans. M.I. Finley (London: Penguin Classics, 1954).

U.S. Census Bureau, *Statistical Abstract of the United States* (Washington, D.C.: Government Printing Office, various years).

Weber, Max. "Politics as a Vocation" in *The Vocation Lectures*, trans. Rodney Livingstone (Indianapolis, IN: Hackett Publishing Company, 2004).

Wright, Robert. *Nonzero, The Logic of Human Destiny* (New York: Vintage Book, 2001).

Xenophon. *Cyropaedia*, trans. Walter Miller (London, Macmillan Company, 1914).

———. *Memorabilia*, trans. Amy L. Bonnette (Cornell: Cornell University Press, 1994).

Young, Julia G. *Mexican Exodus: Emigrants, Exiles and Refugees of the Cristero War* (New York: Oxford University Press, 2015).

Index

About the Authors

MICHAEL GENDRE, PH.D.

Dr. Gendre has taught philosophy, ethics and logic at various colleges in the Boston area, including Boston College, Emerson College, Endicott College, Salem State University and Middlesex Community College. He has translated into English several books from contemporary French philosophical writers, all connected with German philosophy, especially the aftermath of German Idealism and existentialism. He also taught at a private university in Ifrane, Morocco. He obtained his Ph.D. in Philosophy from Boston College, his M.A. at Stanford University, and his B.A. in English at the Université de Provence, Aix-en-Provence, France.

Professor Gendre has published various articles within the field of phenomenology on Hannah Arendt, Heidegger, German Idealism as well as Maurice Merleau-Ponty. He has lectured in France on topics of ancient and modern philosophy, and participated in various international meetings of scholars of phenomenology. His doctoral dissertation was written at Boston College under the guidance of Professors Taminiaux, Cobb-Stevens and Rasmussen. He currently lives in the Boston area.

NICOLÁS SÁNCHEZ, PH.D.

Dr. Sánchez is Professor Emeritus of Economics at The College of the Holy Cross in Worcester, MA. His most recent public achievement was receiving (with co-author Ronald W. Batchelder) the *Duncan Black Prize* for the best economic article published by the *Public Choice Society* in 2013. He is also the co-author of the book (with his former students Christopher Kopp and Francis Sanzari) *Destined for Failure; American Prosperity in the Age of*

Bailouts (Santa Barbara, CA: Praeger, 2010). He was former Chairman of the Economics Department at Holy Cross, and had previously taught at Texas A&M University. He obtained his Ph.D. in Economics from the University of Southern California and his B.A degree from California State Polytechnic University in Pomona, CA.

Professor Sánchez has published many academic articles in his profession, including in *Weltwirtschaftliches Archiv, Cuadernos de Economía, Review of Economics and Statistics, Explorations in Economic History, Economic Development and Cultural Change, American Journal of Agricultural Economics, Journal of Economic Behavior and Organization, Atlantic Economic Journal, Land Economics, Public Choice* and many others. He also published several articles found in book collections, and wrote over 150 articles for the popular press. He currently lives in Fort Lauderdale, FL.